T0145000

Endorsement

I've just spent a wonderful time "walking the streets" of Judy Jane's life. I've laughed with her and sometimes shared her tears; I've gotten to know her family, her friends and her neighbors; I've shared in her successes and failures and sometimes her fears. As I've walked with her, I've heard the "soft sound of sandaled feet"… the presence of Jesus. This is a delightful, refreshing, honest and fun book about normal life that becomes anything but normal because it is life infused with the presence of Christ. Read it and rejoice with me in the "real deal" of what it means to walk with One whose love is without condition and whose grace without measure.

-Steve Brown-
An author, a teacher at Key Life Network and a seminary professor

HEY MOM, #YOUGOTTHIS #HE'SGOTTHIS

120 DAILY INSPIRATIONAL QUIPS

JUDY JANE

WESTBOW
P R E S S®
A DIVISION OF THOMAS NELSON
& ZONDERVAN

Scripture quotations marked NLT are taken from the Holy Bible, New Living Translation, copyright 1996, 2004, 2007. Used by permission of Tyndale House Publishers, Inc. Carol Stream, Illinois 60188. All rights reserved.

Scripture quotations marked MSG are taken from THE MESSAGE. Copyright 1993, 1994, 1995, 1996, 2000, 2001, 2002, 2003 by Eugene H. Peterson. Used by permission of NavPress Publishing Group.

Scripture quotations marked NASB are taken from the New American Standard Bible, Copyright 1960, 1962, 1963, 1968, 1971, 1972, 1973, 1975, 1977, 1995 byThe Lockman Foundation. Used by permission.

Scripture quotations marked NIV are taken from the Holy Bible, New International Version. NIV. Copyright 1973, 1978, 1984 by International Bible Society. Used by permission of Zondervan. All rights reserved.

WestBow Press books may be ordered through booksellers or by contacting:

WestBow Press
A Division of Thomas Nelson & Zondervan
1663 Liberty Drive
Bloomington, IN 47403
www.westbowpress.com
1 (866) 928-1240

Because of the dynamic nature of the Internet, any web addresses or links contained in this book may have changed since publication and may no longer be valid. The views expressed in this work are solely those of the author and do not necessarily reflect the views of the publisher, and the publisher hereby disclaims any responsibility for them.

Any people depicted in stock imagery provided by Thinkstock are models, and such images are being used for illustrative purposes only. Certain stock imagery © Thinkstock.

ISBN: 978-1-5127-8548-7 (sc)
ISBN: 978-1-5127-8546-3 (hc)
ISBN: 978-1-5127-8547-0 (e)

Library of Congress Control Number: 2017906897

Print information available on the last page.

WestBow Press rev. date: 05/08/2017

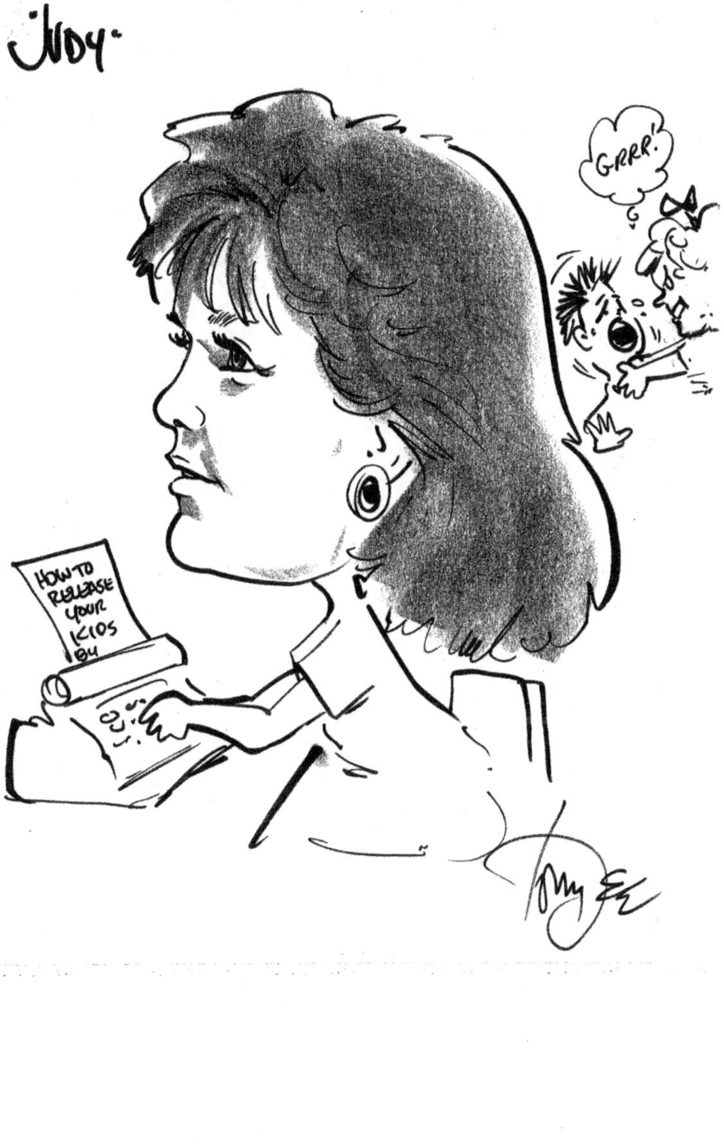
"JUDY"
GRRR!
HOW TO RELEASE YOUR KIDS BY

PREFACE

My parents bought me a five-year diary when I was twelve years old. That's when my love of writing began, as I penned my internal thoughts onto those pages—under lock and key! Of course, the thoughts and subject matter changed as the years went by.

One of my first entries was as follows: "Grandma ate dinner here. I had piano. Grandpa is gone to Michigan, I think painting. I got my first bra, 34AA. Tornado warnings were out!"

I remember that day as if it were yesterday. That was a tumultuous time. Dreaming, learning, and growing, I was trying to figure out my place and purpose in the big world that to an adolescent could at times feel pretty cruel. I continued to write in my diary through the years, and one of my last entries was, "What a day. Ran into Mike S. in front of the teachers college. We are going to start dating again. His arms feel so right being around me again! I love him!"

We were married shortly after that, in August of 1974, and I did some feature writing for a couple of daily newspapers before we started our family. My writing continued as I wrote all about being a mom to three boys and a daughter. I absolutely loved being a mom—even though it made for long days, messy clothes (both theirs and mine), lack of sleep, lots of cooking, an untidy house, and lots of noise.

There are so many different stages of motherhood. As the child is growing and changing, it is inevitable that Mom changes along with them. There is the infancy stage and all that brings; and then come the toddler years, the school years, the junior high years, the high school years, the post-high school years, and the adult years. Yes, even when your children are adults you don't stop being a mom. My mom, who is in her late eighties, still wants me to call when my sixty-four-year-old husband and my sixty-two-year-old self are coming back from a trip, so she can make sure we've arrived home safely. Once a mom, always a mom.

120

This particular number came up a lot when our youngest two boys were teens and spending a lot of time fishing. The two boys and one of their friends would go around speaking in silly teen language: "Yep ... 120 ... sweet." This went on for days on end throughout one particular summer. I kept asking what it meant, and they would not share with me. So I decided to start saying, "Yep ... 2006 ... sweet." My strategy worked. It drove them just as crazy as they had been driving me crazy! They finally couldn't stand it any longer and insisted I tell them.

I said, "Okay, you go first!"

They said, "Well, it is the depth of the water where we are catching mahi-mahi. So, Mom, what is 2006?"

I replied, "Well, it is the year that the last of you will graduate and be out of here!" So it became a family joke between our two youngest boys, and I kept seeing the number 120 come up in lots of other circumstances—including in scripture! The number was used to describe the end of humanity's days in Noah's time (Genesis 6:3–4). Moses lived for 120 years (Deuteronomy 34:5–7), 120 priests sounded trumpets at the dedication of Solomon's temple (2 Chronicles 5:13–14), and on the day of Pentecost there were 120 in the upper room (Acts 1:15). From what I read and from my limited understanding (I'm not a theologian or a numerologist), it seems to symbolize a divinely appointed time of waiting, speaking of the second coming of the Lord Jesus Christ. Since I know that scripture makes it clear that humanity will not know the hour that Jesus will return (Matthew 24:36), I choose not to concern myself with that. What it does show me is that God's promises are true and that it will come to pass that He will return in His perfect timing. The number continues to come up, and the last time was on a day when one of our sons bought a new home. In his new address was the number 120!

Fishers of Men

My father-in-law passed down to my husband and his brother a passion for fishing, and the two of them passed this love of the outdoors and this hobby down to their children. Our greatest desire and prayer is that they will have an even greater passion for becoming "fishers of men."

I grew up in Sunday school learning the song "Fishers of Men," which was based on Mark 1:17 (NLT): "Come, follow me, and I will show you how to fish for people!" The song went like this:

I will make you fishers of men,
Fishers of men, fishers of men.
I will make you fishers of men,
If you follow me.

If you follow me,
If you follow me,
I will make you fishers of men,
If you follow me.

Hear Christ calling, "Come unto me,
Come unto me, come unto me."
Hear Christ calling, "Come unto me,
And I will give you rest."

As I was working on this chapter, the doorbell rang; it was my neighbor's son asking if he could fish off the dock in our backyard. I was reminded of the Bill and Gloria Gaither song I used to listen to and sing to my boys when they were small, "God Loves To Talk To Little Boys When They're Fishin'"

I so miss my boys hanging out and fishing and bringing home the fresh fish! So I was excited when the neighbors wanted to hang out on the dock. I even hung out with them for a while, but then I left them alone so that they could "listen."

These are the lyrics.

God speaks to little boys while they're fishin';
That seems to be the time boys listen best.
It's the only quiet time there is for wishin';
It's the only time when God and boys can rest.

There's something about a boy who's good at fishin';
God knows he'll make a very special friend.
A boy who learns to listen while he's fishin'
Can hear God when it's time to fish for men.

A Prayer for My Children

This devotion is written in hopes of encouraging parents in all stages of parenting. Parenting isn't a piece of cake; the title of one of my favorite books by Dr. James Dobson concurs, *Parenting Isn't for Cowards*. The culture we live in is changing at an alarming pace. The pressures our children and grandchildren are facing are unlike any that we faced when we were younger.

My children are quite proficient in rigging a line and catching a fish, and it has kept them and their families in food at times. But my prayer is—and will be until I take my last breath—that they will be just as sensitive to the small, still voice of their Creator. I hope they will respond and desire to fulfill the great commission of fishing for men just as earnestly as they listen to the sound of a fish taking the bait and feel the pull of their line.

I would like them to go out and tell the world, "People do not live by bread alone; rather, we live by every word that comes from the mouth of the Lord" (Deuteronomy 8:3 NLT).

A New Kind of Fisherman

Walking along the beach of Lake Galilee, Jesus saw two brothers—Simon (who was later called Peter) and Andrew. They were fishing and throwing their nets into the lake. It was their regular work.

Jesus said to them, "Come with Me. I will make a new kind of fisherman out of you. I'll show you how to catch men and women instead of perch and bass." They didn't ask questions; they simply dropped their nets and followed.

A short distance down the beach, they came upon another pair of brothers, James and John. These two were sitting in a boat with their father, Zebedee, and mending their nets. Jesus made the same offer to them, and they were just as quick to follow; they abandoned both their boat and their father (Matthew 4:18–22 MSG).

I have one son who is on the water for a living, and we have prayed for his safety through many storms. I have also prayed that God would reveal Himself through His creation to this particular son.

> Some of you set sail in big ships; you put to sea to do business in faraway ports … Out at sea you saw God in action, saw his breathtaking ways with the ocean: With a word he called up the wind—an ocean storm, towering waves! You shot high in the sky, then the bottom dropped out; your hearts were stuck in your throats. You were spun like a top, you reeled like a drunk, and you didn't know which end was up. Then you called out to God in your

desperate condition; he got you out in the nick of time. He quieted the wind down to a whisper, put a muzzle on all the big waves. And you were so glad when the storm died down and he led you safely back to harbor. So thank God for his marvelous love, for his miracle mercy to the children he loves. Lift high your praises when the people assemble; shout Hallelujah when the elders meet! (Psalm 107:23–32 MSG)

The love of a mother is so strong that it is difficult to put into words. But it doesn't even compare to the love our Lord has for us. Yes, our heavenly Father loves our children more than we are capable of, and it is to Him that we must turn. We must ask Him to do a work in their lives.

We have our children for a short span—to love, to teach, and to train. After that, part of our job—the most difficult part—is to let go. We have to let go and hopefully watch them make wonderful choices and be encouraged. But sometimes we must watch them live out the lifelong consequences of poor decisions.

Wherever you are in your walk as a mother—whether you're a new mom, a mom in deep pain because of your child's choices, or a mom whose relationship with her child feels damaged beyond repair—take hope and be reminded that we have all sinned and fall short of the glory of God. But He has made a way for us to be reconciled to Him.

A youth pastor at our church took us to a Youth for Christ teen conference in 1970. An entry was made in my diary on December 29. I was sixteen years old.

"I became a Christian at HTC (Holiday Teen Conference) in Chicago. Ken Poure helped me! The rooms are gorgeous! Ken Poure spoke to us, and he told us how to become Christians. I thought I was, but I discovered that I wasn't. I personally asked Jesus Christ into my heart! The happiest day of my life."

I don't know if I have spelled Ken's name correctly—and I can't after all of these years even put a face to his name! But Ken had a spirit for young people, and God used him to speak to the heart of a young sixteen-year-old girl who was delighted to hear that God was more than just a distant being. I learned that day that He was a God who created me, knew me, and cared for me. Thank you, Ken, for investing in my life.

I have since then googled Ken's name, and as I write this, I have a face to put with his name. I learned that God has continued to use him to reach young people through Christian camps. As soon as I heard his voice on the Internet, I recognized it, along with his humor and enthusiasm. God used all those gifts that He created in Ken to speak to me that December day in 1970, and I will be forever grateful.

After all these years (forty-two, to be exact), I clicked on a message from this same man who God used to begin my faith walk, and I was encouraged and reminded that this life isn't what it's all about. I was reminded that our story of salvation isn't finished until we are complete in Christ, which will happen upon our deaths.

Let Go of Regret

If you have regrets, let them go. I have none. In spite of the difficult times, I wouldn't change a thing about the family that we were loaned. I am who I am today because of the challenges that having my particular family brought my way.

Maybe I could have gone on with my writing career, or been a part of changing the height requirements so that I could be an airline flight attendant, or traveled internationally with my husband—who turned down that opportunity so we could all be together as a family.

None of that compares with the blessing of raising a family of four with the love of my life, my greatest earthly encourager, my husband Michael. He, for some reason, fell in love with me when

I was sixteen years old and vowed at the young age of twenty-one years to love me through better or worse. We have seen better and we have seen worse, but he is still my greatest encourager and my cheerleader, who has chosen to love me unconditionally. For that I am forever grateful.

My heart is heavy right now for the grief that my brother and sister-in-law are experiencing, as they have just walked through the first year after losing their son, Preston, to suicide. He was just short of fourteen years old when he died. His mom and I have talked through the years about the ups and downs of parenting, but this most recent tragedy has reminded us in a dramatic way that this really isn't our home. We believe that my nephew understood oh-so-well that it wasn't his home and that he was longing for heaven.

The story of our salvation isn't complete until we take our last breaths. In the meantime we have pangs, just as in childbirth.

> When a woman gives birth, she has a hard time; there's no getting around it. But when the baby is born, there is joy in the birth. This new life in the world wipes out memory of the pain. The sadness you have right now is similar to that pain, but the coming joy is also similar. When I see you again, you'll be full of joy, and it will be a joy no one can rob from you. You'll no longer be so full of questions. This is what I want you to do: Ask the Father for whatever is in keeping with the things I've revealed to you. Ask in my name, according to my will, and he'll most certainly give it to you. Your joy will be a river overflowing its banks! (John 16:21–22 MSG)

As you're reading these quips throughout your days, be in prayer for your children and grandchildren. Look up the scriptures to see how God will speak to you through them. I hope that you will be encouraged and comforted when you see some of the things that our family has lived through. Thanks for all that you do as a mom and be reminded that "there is no higher calling than raising the children God has entrusted to your care." (Dr. James Dobson, author)

To my beloved children and grandchildren, and to anyone else who might feel spoken to through these writings, if you haven't already, drop your nets and follow Him.

CHAPTER 1

YOUNGER DAYS

#FiveSecondRule

There is a time for everything, and a season for every activity under heaven: a time to weep and a time to laugh.

—Ecclesiastes 3:1&4 (NIV)

I was fixing dinner one summer evening, after a full day of cleaning and doing laundry. We had just returned from a vacation with our family of six—seven including our yellow Lab.

The kids were sitting at the table in the eat-in area and just talking and horsing around as I finished up the meal. As I was working in front of the stove, I suddenly felt a pain in my right upper arm. Startled, I looked up, and I felt at the same time a splash of water on my leg. I discovered that I had just had a banana ricochet off me and into the dog's water bowl!

As soon as he could catch his breath from his guffawing, the first thing out of my son's mouth was "Don't worry, Mom, I'll eat it!"

I had to stifle myself from bursting into laughter. It might have led to anarchy, and I would never again have been in control! My kids, of course, knew me too well, and they started urging me, "Mom, don't smile!"

I am always so confused about what a "proper" mom response is or whether I should just give in to my instincts to laugh at the insanity of it all.

Part of me wants to get in there with them and start throwing bananas, while the "mature" part of me tells me that I will live to regret it. So I usually end up somewhere in between, with the kids getting the last laugh as they watch me attempt to exercise self- control.

Lord, thank You for families and, yes, for the insanity of living in a large family! Thank You for helping me with self-control and for the wisdom needed to know when it is okay to just laugh along with them!

#Community

A friend is always loyal, and a brother is born to help in time of need.

—Proverbs 17:17 (NIV)

When we started our family in the late seventies and eighties, my husband and I together decided that I would be a stay-at-home mom while we were raising our children. That meant that I would give up my newspaper career to become a full-time mom.

I was more than willing and actually excited about the opportunity to be a stay-at-home mom. Believe it or not, even at that time stay-at-home moms were becoming the exception rather than the norm.

Luckily for me, there were three young families on our street who had moms at home, so I had a huge support system in place. We didn't live in the neighborhood that we would have preferred, or drive the car that we would have liked to, or have a designer home. But we found this decision workable for us and less stressful than if we had both been working. Looking back, I see it was the perfect neighborhood for us and the perfect decision.

The moms in our "hood" patrolled our children as they played in the street together. We nursed our babies together on the front porch swings, we listened to baby monitors as older children were picked up from school, and, if any one of us were losing it, we had an open-door policy to watch her children to give her a cooling down period. We took each other up on it, too. We shared our lives. We talked about the good and the bad and the ugly, and we cried on each other's shoulders. It was truly a community, and I was grateful for it.

With the huge changes in technology, I have wondered if young moms today feel isolated. I know phone calls among friends seem to be rarer as texting has become the prominent method of communicating. I get it that texting is easier in many ways, but I also know firsthand the mental health benefits of being able to connect voice to voice or, even better, face to face with a friend. We are connecting, but I fear that our method of communicating is leading to isolation and discouragement.

As I write this I have three men in my future kitchen, installing the wiring that will eventually bring me the necessary light for my workspace. Some are hammering, some are pulling wire, and others are cutting through concrete. It is loud and, at times, contentious. There is much communication going on, all necessary to get the job done. It has been fun to see them working tenaciously toward a common goal. It reminds me of the way that moms, no matter what our age, work together to raise our children.

I wrote these quips because I value the role of moms in our society and I wish to be a cheerleader to all moms. I loved being a mom, but I also know that it can seem at times to be an exhausting, thankless, nerve-wracking, dirty, unfulfilling, exasperating, never-ending job that comes with no monetary compensation.

I was reminded of this recently when we vacationed with our daughter and son-in-law and their then three-year-old daughter and seventeen-month-old son. Our kitchen was under construction, so she had offered to take care of a lot of the food, which required planning, shopping, and packing while caring for two toddlers—no easy task! We arrived at the rental house, and while unloading and trying to put things away, she was also attempting to give medicine to one of the children, who was being uncooperative. I heard a loud sound, which I thought was laughter but soon discovered to be a wail of sorts. I found her on the bed, having a meltdown. I tried to listen between the sobs. "Why does this have to be so hard?" I felt inept at trying to comfort her and just tried to listen and assure her that we were there to help and that we would enjoy being together whether the children cooperated or not. I remembered vacations we had taken and the expectations I'd had, and I understood.

I'm so thankful that my daughter has found a close friend in her neighborhood. My husband and I are far away, so we can't be as much help as we'd like to be. A support system is so important in getting through not just the toddler years but life in general. Joining a women's Bible study group in your local church, seeking out other young moms in your neighborhood, looking to meet others through MOPS (Mothers of Preschoolers) groups, and joining a couples small group are all ways to get through the tough days of motherhood and life in general. We were not designed to do this mothering thing—or life—alone. The friends that I made when my children were small are some of the best friends I still have.

So why we would be willing to take on such a tough job? We have to go back to truth. Scripture tells us our children are a gift. "Don't you see that children are God's best gift? The fruit of the womb his generous legacy? Like a warrior's fistful of arrows are the children of a vigorous youth. Oh, how blessed are you parents, with your quivers full of children." Psalm 127:3–4 (MSG)

Mom, enjoy the gift or gifts you have been given, and ask the Lord to give you strength and wisdom in raising them. Our culture will never applaud your efforts, and your children may not either, but the Father who gave you these gifts sees.

Dear Lord, I thank You for the friends that I have had throughout the years, while raising our family and beyond. You knew exactly which neighborhood we should be in throughout all the different stages of life and encouraged us with just the neighbors we were supposed to have. I am grateful that You didn't intend for us to be lone soldiers but designed us to need one another.

#EyesonYou

Likewise, teach the older women to be reverent in the way they live, not to be slanderers or addicted to much wine but to teach what is good. They then can train the younger women to love their husbands and children, to be self-controlled and pure, to be busy at home, to be kind, and to be subject to their husbands, so that no one will malign the word of God.

—Titus 2:6 (NIV)

When is the last time that you stayed home for an entire day and listened to nothing but quietness? I had a day like that recently. I caught up with my laundry and even did some mending; now, that is something we don't do much anymore. There is something about sewing on buttons and hemming pants that produces such a feeling of accomplishment.

I have had older women in my life from the time I can remember, and I have always enjoyed watching and listening to them. Many ministered to me when I was a small child and teenager in the church family that I grew up in. Then, as I grew up, I had older women who encouraged me along the way as I was raising small children, and God also placed a special woman in my life to walk with me as I was raising teens.

Now that I'm an "older" woman myself, I have felt that young moms really aren't interested in what we older ones have learned along the way. As I was working around the house, I came to understand

5

that the older generation I was among was teaching me, and I just didn't realize it. Maybe today's young moms, in their busyness, are like me. They, too, don't recognize that they are learning, but they are, and one day it will have new meaning to them, as well.

I played while my mom and her friends darned socks, sewed on buttons, and hand-stitched hems, but I didn't realize at the time that their lifestyle was something that I could learn from. Much more was going on in that sewing group than sewing. Life was being shared, problems were being worked through, and mundane but necessary tasks were being accomplished—all while they helped each other through life.

My mom used to sing a song that she learned at camp when she was small. The words describe a much simpler time. I think there is something to say for the routines of life. It is during the routines that children watch and learn.

> Today is Sunday, today is Sunday,
> Sunday, church.
> Saturday, payday;
> Friday, fish;
> Thursday, roast beef;
> Wednesday, sou-oup!
> Tuesday, string beans;
> Monday, wash day.
> Everybody happy? Well, I should smile!

I did learn from the older women. I learned from many that they found great joy in serving their husbands by cooking and washing and mending. Perhaps there was something to staying at home and being content with being a homemaker and caregiver of their families.

Mom, I may not have said anything, but I want you to know that I was watching and learning, and I grew up desiring what you had. I watched you raise us, that being your first priority after your relationship with Dad. I watched you put Dad's paycheck into envelopes, and I saw one marked "our tithe." I watched you make Sunday morning about worshipping and Sunday afternoons about visiting the lonely—when you could pull Dad away from the golf matches! And I watched you entertain to encourage others.

As we left the nest, I watched your focus change from us to getting involved in helping others. I saw you volunteer in the mission downtown. I saw your care for the homebound and sick. I saw you support your friends through the ups and downs of life, and I saw you continue to make your husband your priority. I saw you grow in your marriage relationship because of that commitment. I learned that church wasn't just for kids.

Dear Lord, I thank You for my mom and the other older women in my life, who helped me through the different stages in my childhood and as an adult. Now I am an older adult myself. I thank You for the way you use others to encourage us and to teach us, many times without us realizing it until years later. Thank You for giving me contentedness in being home at this new stage of life, something that I'd thought would be difficult. Help me to accept this new stage of life, which is quieter and, well, more routine. Help me be one of those older women who will be an encouragement to younger moms as they listen and observe. Thank You for your faithfulness in showing me how You desire for me to spend my time through each new season of life.

#FessUp

Make this your common practice: Confess your sins to each other and pray for each other so that you can live together whole and healed. The prayer of a person living right with God is something powerful to be reckoned with.

—James 5:16 (MSG)

We, as humans, usually try to take the easy way out, but hopefully we learn as we grow in wisdom that what we perceive as the "easy way" may indeed be the more difficult path. I was reminded of this as our third child, our second-oldest son, was in a recovery room, waking up after surgery on his hand.

He had mentioned to us, months prior, that he had removed a fish hook from his hand. After looking at it, we were able to see that an infection had developed, so we took him to a doctor so he could get an antibiotic. Months later, he complained of a cyst on that same hand, so we took him back to the doctor. He advised that the cyst should be surgically removed and that a general anesthesia would be necessary because of all the nerve endings in the hand.

After the surgery, the doctor found me in the waiting room and asked me if I would like to see what they'd discovered. The "cyst" was not a cyst at all but a copper BB!

When I saw my son in the recovery room, I asked him whether he'd heard what the doctor had removed from his hand and whether he was surprised. He admitted that he had been playing with his BB gun up in his room, shooting spit wads. Wanting to see how hard a spit wad would shoot out of the gun, he had pointed it at his hand! He said he didn't know that there were any BBs in the gun and was surprised when one shot out. I'm not sure whether this was before or after his hunter's training course! I told him that surely he'd seen an entry hole, but he said, "No, but it did bleed a lot!"

This cyst-like thing on his hand had been as hard as a rock and painful to touch. Isn't it true that we often choose to take what we think will be the road of least resistance in an effort to avoid pain? It is always so obvious with children, but don't we as adults do exactly the same thing? I'm sure he was hesitant to tell us at the time what he had done, because he knew we would be upset with him. He knew that playing around, even with a BB gun, without Dad being present was forbidden. He had thought that by not mentioning it he could avoid a lot of pain. Had he told us, we could have either tried to remove it ourselves or the doctor could have easily removed it at that point.

Instead it stayed in his hand, where the body tried to reject it, but to no avail. That increased the pain, and more pain would be required to fix the situation.

Our problems, too, get worse. They fester and eventually abscess if we don't face the music and deal with them head on.

Lord, help me to remember this example as I am tempted to take the "easy" way out to avoid all sorts of perceived pain and embarrassment in my life.

#ImaBadMom

For I am the Lord your God who takes hold of your right hand and says to you, Do not fear; I will help you.

—Isaiah 41:13 (NIV)

Our fourth child had been born, and we had started to settle in with our new routine. We had received much help from my parents, who stayed with our other three children while I was in the hospital and continued their stay to help while we were all adjusting to our, now, family of six.

The wonderful, helpful meals from our church family had ended, my parents had gone home, my husband was back to work, and I was now on my own—with the exception of four children: an eight-year-old, a six-year-old, a three-year-old, and a newborn.

I had decided that I couldn't put off any longer a trip to the

9

grocery store, as we were out of the necessities. The thought of taking all four to the store for the first time was intimidating, but I was up for the challenge, or so I thought! I was thinking to myself, in today's lingo, *I've got this!*

So I loaded everyone up, secured them, and headed to the shopping center. We made it inside, and the baby slept in his infant seat in the bottom of the cart as I shopped. Feeling thankful that I had made it through the experience with the baby never waking, I felt as if everything were under control. All that I had left to do was check out!

This grocery setup was such that you would take your cart to the left, so the cashier could remove the items from her side, and then you would go to the right, where you would finish your transaction.

That is when things started to fall apart. I remember all three of the children speaking to me at once and asking for my individual attention. I was just trying to finish up and get out as quickly as I could before things went from bad to worse. I tried to be the in-control mom and speak softly to the children, explaining that I was trying to check out and that it was important for them to hold their questions until we were finished. This was pre debit-card times, so I removed my checkbook as I waited for the total. The transaction complete, I remember grabbing the hand of our three-year-old, hoping to get all three of them across the parking lot to the vehicle in one piece and then getting everyone in, while an employee helped me load the groceries. It was then that I suddenly realized that I had all the children and the groceries—but I didn't have my baby!

I panicked when I realized that our infant son had been left in the grocery store! I looked at the poor bag boy and yelled, "Where is my baby!"

I remember him just looking at me and politely saying, "I don't know where your baby is, ma'am." I then asked the boy to stay with the other three children and, without waiting for his answer, ran back into the store!

I ran to the cashier, who didn't seem to know where the baby was. I scanned the area but did not see a cart with a baby carrier in it. I quickly looked at all the carts that were stacked up together in a line, and at last I caught a glimpse of white that resembled the infant seat.

I started pulling those carts out one by one, until I reached the cart where my precious baby was still fast asleep. To this day I have no idea how that cart ended up in the middle of all the other carts without someone noticing my baby! But I was beyond relieved, so it didn't matter.

Adrenaline pumping, I loaded my baby into the car, with visions of what could have been running through my head. Once I got home, with all of us safe and sound, I called my husband, crying. I confessed what a bad mom that I was and vowed never to go to the grocery store alone, ever again!

Oh, Lord, I thank You for protecting our baby today, even when I didn't. I can see that this job is way too big for me to navigate on my own. I need Your help.

#HouseofHorror

> I needed clothes and you clothed me, I was sick and you looked after me, I was in prison and you came to visit me.
>
> —Matthew 25:36 (NIV)

After driving through flatlands and cornfields, we arrived at an ominous three-story nursing home in Indiana, to visit my grandmother, my children's great-grandmother.

What transpired could through the eyes of a nine-year-old be every bit as frightening as a late-night horror movie!

We walked up the steps to the home, past a reception area and past the smiling greetings of the youngest, most capable convalescents. These people turned to stare at the new arrivals with a curiosity-based welcome. "Come in! We're so glad to see you!"

We made our way past these initial wanderers unscathed and headed to the big black elevator to the third floor, which my son said smelled like "oatmeal and old people mixed!"

It was almost lunchtime, so there was a bustle of activity. We wove our way through the hallways filled with lined-up wheelchairs and walkers, hoping we wouldn't be grabbed by a wandering hand. Through the maze, to Grandmother's room we went.

We passed a group of elderly people in exercise class, which amounted to a stuffed ball being tossed and a geriatric version of the game duck, duck, goose. Some ladies were getting their nails manicured in the hallway, some were singing to themselves while catatonically rocking, some were blurting out obscenities, and one man was screaming, "Someone get me, get me, a drink *now!*" We walked past another room, where a man had his pants half off, and was screaming, "Help, help! Somebody help me!"

To the great relief of the children, we finally reached my grandma's room. As we visited, I noticed that they kept their backs to the wall and eyes on the doorway at all times; I assumed it was out of nervousness in case of any of the residents had decided to follow them!

As we were saying our goodbyes in the corridor, a little woman in a wheelchair, who appeared sweet enough, started cooing to my one son as he walked by her. She put her hand out to him, with an endearing, "Come here, little bo-o-oy." My unsuspecting son hesitated but sauntered toward her with an I-should-be-nice-to-this-woman look. He trustingly reached his hand out to hers and gazed into her distorted, wrinkled face.

Just as he did, she lunged forward, grabbing his arm with both of hers, and wrapped her thankfully toothless gums around his arm! She then quickly released her grip, wheeled her chair around, and continued on down the hall, convulsing with laughter!

We all laughed at the look of horror on my son's face. The little woman had gotten the best of us that day!

My son apparently lost a lot of trust for people that day, and I can't say I blame him. But he also learned to laugh as he recalled the story of the "vicious, gross" woman in that nursing home.

I don't think any of us will forget that day. In fact, I'll probably pounce upon some unsuspecting little boy myself someday, if I ever wind up convalescing in such a home. I'm sure it will turn an otherwise dull day into one to celebrate!

Dear Lord, I pray that my children will remember visiting my grandmother during some of the final days of her life. They didn't know and love my grandmother the way I did, but I pray that they will find joy in stepping out of their comfort zones to minister to others who need encouragement. I hope they will understand or come to an understanding that while they are serving others they are serving You.

#LeftBehind

> Humble yourselves, therefore, under God's mighty hand, that he may lift you up in due time. Cast all your anxiety on him because he cares for you.
>
> —1 Peter 5:6–7 (NIV)

I really hesitated when deciding whether or not to share this story. But I decided that there are plenty of mothers who have experienced some pretty embarrassing toddler moments, and who knows, I just might encourage one mom!

I was a first-time mom of a two-year-old son when I did something that I could never have imagined I would stoop to!

I clearly remember wanting to get out of the house. I had been busy attempting to toilet-train my firstborn, in hopes of having him trained before we brought his sister home in a few short months.

We had tried everything. I had even foolishly bought a book that said it could be done in one day! In an effort to help, his grandmother had mailed special "big-boy" pants with his favorite characters on them in hopes of making him want to discard the diapers. I was ready to buy stock in the M&M's company, as we were going through so many of them! He'd sit on the toilet and eat them, but he wouldn't do anything else.

His birthday was imminent, so I decided to take a trip out to a nearby toy store to get some ideas of what he might be interested in—and also to while away some time. I had read that short little outings were a good testing ground.

We had gone through several aisles, and everything was going smoothly—no pun intended—until I smelled something that wasn't a usual toy store smell. It was then I realized that my toddler had made the decision to take care of business right in the middle of the aisle! Let's just say he left a deposit on the floor.

Thankfully, there were several aisles, and I was in one that was empty for the moment. I was horrified! I didn't know what to do. I didn't have anything to clean it up with, and I was way too young and embarrassed to go to the clerk and admit what had happened, or so I thought. So I did what any respectable, responsible twenty-six-year-old mom of a toddler would do—I panicked! I picked up that boy so fast he didn't know what had happened, walked toward the door, and even had the nerve to thank the clerk for her help. I plopped my son into his car seat in record time and drove away in my getaway car!

Lord, we worry way too much about what others think. Forgive me for leaving that mess for some unsuspecting employee to discover today. Who knows, I might have met a new friend had I been honest and up front about what had transpired. Maybe we could even have had a good laugh together. Forgive me for not trusting You and just running out instead of dealing with my responsibility.

#Punked

A time to weep and a time to laugh.

—Ecclesiastes 3:4 (NIV)

Snakes and snails and puppy dog tails is touted as what little boys are made of, but as a mother of three boys, I say worms is more accurate—pinworms, in particular.

You may be reading this and be the mother of a boy and have never experienced pinworms. If so, then you may have made it through your parenthood journey ignorant of the fact that your son had them, or you might have lived in a sterile environment and never let your son outside to play in the dirt. Actually, they are not at all exclusive to boys, but I blamed my boys for infecting my daughter and myself because I can't imagine that she or I could have been capable of being a carrier!

When my children were young and became exceptionally hyper or were scratching, it was time for a pinworm inspection. Squeamishness and motherhood do not mix. A call to the doctor the next morning, and he would prescribe some "wormy" pills to kill the parasites. The entire family has to be treated to avoid reinfection.

A daily changing of all bed sheets is necessary, and frequent dusting to get all the eggs that are floating around home sweet home lessens the possibility of reinfection. But don't go too crazy, because the eggs can even be floating around in the air, and you can inhale them. Just do the best you can, and be sure to finish all of your medication.

When one of my sons was exceptionally hyper one week, I decided it was time for him to be checked out. My husband attributed his hyperactivity to his age, but I was sure the infamous pin worms were responsible. Upon the nighttime inspection, to my shock, I got a glimpse of the biggest pin worm I had ever seen! What I saw were two "purple grape green glitter" plastic fishing worms. It was a classic parent moment; we laughed until we cried at our son's creativity. We had been "punked!"

My son got our attention that night with his sense of humor, and he'll never have to worry about us checking him again!

Lord, thanks for laughter. Help us not to take life so seriously and to look for opportunities to laugh. Thank You for the children You have loaned to us and for the laughter they bring into our lives.

#WhatsThatSmell

> A cheerful disposition is good for your health;
> gloom and doom leave you bone-tired.
>
> —Proverbs 17:22 (MSG)

Noticing one day that our dog had a worse-than-usual odor, I started trying to determine from where the smell was originating. I started with her breath and then examined her ears, eliminating different body parts as I went. I finally narrowed the pungent smell down to her posterior. Surprising, huh?

After I mentioned it to my neighbor, he proceeded to tell me about a dog he'd had with a particular gland that was the source of an intense odor. I went online and found a site which talked of this gland. It described step by step how a pet owner could try to take care of the problem—a major downside of the Internet! I shared the information with my husband, who quickly said he wasn't up for it! He then offered our fifteen-year-old twenty dollars to do the dirty deed.

Excited with the thought that he could make twenty dollars that quickly, our son ran to the garage to get some rubber gloves to prepare for the procedure. We all discussed our particular roles. My husband would hold the head, I was to hold the tail up, and our son was instructed to do his job.

We took our assigned places as we prepared for the procedure, with the garden hose ready for what might exit. We watched as our son tried to muster up the courage to make the plunge, and the watching turned into uncontrollable laughter. His face was red with laughter as he tried to talk himself into the feat, and my husband's face was distorted as he took in the insanity of the entire situation. Both of us were laughing in amazement that our son would do this for a mere twenty dollars, but now he was renegotiating to up the ante to thirty dollars!

The laughter continued during the entire process. We were all quite surprised that the dog not only didn't seem to be experiencing any discomfort but was, amazingly, quite calm.

Lord, thank You for families and for laughter in the midst of the not-so-pleasant routines that are part of our lives.

CHAPTER 2

GIFT OF FRIENDSHIP

#AppleofMyEye

He calls his own sheep by name.

—John 10:3 (MSG)

Two of my sons had gone up to Georgia one September to do some bow hunting. They were staying with some extremely generous good friends who open their home to one of our sons quite often when he takes a break from being on tugboats.

After a recent visit, my sons got back in town and stopped by to share their provision of venison meat and two bags of apples that their friend's wife had packaged and sent for us. I was so excited! Septembers in Florida have little resemblance to the falls that I remember up north; of all the seasons, I miss the fall the most. Trips to the apple orchard were one of my favorite childhood memories, picking the apples and then enjoying a glass of freshly squeezed apple cider.

I was so touched, as it was such a thoughtful thing to do, but I was really moved when I realized that she had taken the time to write the names of the varieties of apple on each bag and written my name, "Mrs. Sap." It is a shorter version of my name, and I found that even more endearing. Gift-giving is one of my "love languages," which is also why it spoke to me so much. (This refers to the book *The 5 Love Languages*, by Gary Chapman.)

I was reminded how we all like to be recognized by our names and how I really need to work at that. I know it means so much when you do remember and call someone by name. I will no longer just accept that I'm really bad at remembering names. I will make a conscious effort to learn and call people by their names.

Dear Lord, thank You so much for friends. Thank You for Mike and Tiff, for their friendship to our sons, and for their thoughtfulness. Thank You for calling us by name and referring to us as *the apples of your eye* to describe the depth of love You have for Your children.

#CoffeeTime

As for God, his way is perfect; the word of the Lord is flawless.

—Psalm 18:30 (NIV)

My favorite time of the morning is when I get to sit down with my coffee and my best friend to learn more about Him.

The best friend I am referring to is Jesus. Before you dismiss me as being "a few peas short of a casserole," let me explain. I am a people person and would prefer to be with others, but after raising four children and having gained some maturation with a few added years, I have learned to be quite okay with quiet. In fact, it is not only my favorite time of the morning; I have also come to depend on it. I want to know how to order my day so I don't miss something that He may have for me to do.

The Bible is described as being alive and God-breathed. When you have asked Christ into your life, you are indwelled with the Holy Spirit, who is a comfort and guide to people.

While it is not an audible voice—beware if someone tells you it is—it is a thought that goes through your head, and *if* the thought lines up with scripture, you can be sure that it is the voice of God. If it does not line up with God's word, then you have to question where this other voice is coming from. So He speaks through the written word that He left us.

I have a coffee mug which I purchased so I could enjoy my coffee in a decorative cup. It's a girl thing! I hadn't used the cup for a while, since a friend who was helping me wash dishes accidently chipped it on the sink. She felt bad, and I assured her it was no big deal, especially since I enjoy shopping for little things like that.

I had it in my cupboard but had chosen not to keep it displayed any longer because of the flaw in it. I thought about that cup this morning and decided to drag it out and start using it just as it is, chip and all. This will be a reminder of how I am first, a chip off the ole block, as my earthly dad used to say, but as a reminder that outside of Christ I am flawed. "While we were still sinners, Christ died for us" (Romans 5:8).

Lord, thank You for the reminder that Your word, the word of God, is the only thing in this world that is flawless. Forgive me for the times that I fall into the trap of self-sufficiency and go about my personal agenda. Yes, even the fact that I woke up this morning is because of you. Help me to not miss what You have for me today.

#DowntoDetails

God, investigate my life; get all the facts firsthand. I'm an open book to you; even from a distance, you know what I'm thinking. You know when I leave and when I get back; I'm never out of your sight. You know everything I'm going to say before I start the first sentence. I look behind me, and You're there, then up ahead, and You're there, too. Your reassuring presence, coming and going. This is too much, too wonderful ... I can't take it all in!"

—Psalm 139:1–6 (MSG)

When talking with skeptics, I've heard the comment that they get irritated when people talk about situations they are in and how God has met their needs—such as empty gas tanks that get them to their destinations, etc. I was scoffed at when I said that I absolutely think that God cares about the littlest details in our lives.

The night before this conversation, a dear elderly friend of ours missed a step and fell. I was in front of her and my husband behind her. It happened so quickly that, unfortunately, neither of us were able to break her fall. We couldn't get out of our heads the sound of her head hitting the concrete. She lost consciousness for about thirty seconds, but after coming to, she appeared to be okay. We all tried to encourage her to go to the hospital for an x-ray of her head, but she refused. Three of us sat at her home to make sure she was going to be okay, and we planned to stay with her overnight so that she would not be alone. Her brother, who lived next door, said he would stay with her. She was at church the next morning, and tears ran down her face as she sang along with one of the worship songs these words: "Look what the Lord has done for me." She knew that God had, for whatever reason, mercifully spared her from deeper injuries. She had even fallen on a shoulder that had recently been broken, and her shoulder was still intact.

The weekend before, my husband and I had met up with a childhood girlfriend of mine and her husband. We had specifically prayed together for our husbands from the time we were teens. We lived on opposite ends of the country for years, but we have stayed in touch. When our husbands met each other for the first time, there were some interesting similarities in their personalities, demeanor, and interests. They also "happened" to share the same first name. When we were together this time, her father-in-law "happened" to call while we were together, and I noticed the name Norman show up on caller ID. I asked, "Is that Mike's dad's name?" My friend said yes, that's where Mike had gotten his middle name. We couldn't believe it! We were both learning that our husbands, whom we had prayed for together over forty years ago, not only shared the same first name but, we were learning at this moment, also had their middle names in common! I believe that, if for no other reason than to encourage both of us at that stage of life, God had heard and answered those simple little prayers of two young girls. Our faith had been the size of a mustard seed; we'd believed that God was a personal God who would lead us to men who wanted to live for the Lord rather than themselves. We were encouraged and reminded at this moment that our prayers today are every bit as powerful, and while the world is changing at alarming rates, the God who we trusted in is still trustworthy.

Thank you, Lord, for being the God of the Universe and a God of amazing details. Your Creation is evidence of Your obvious attention to detail, and You have personally shown me that You care about everything that is of concern to me. You know how Your people are encouraged by evidence of You working in the little things as well as the big. Lord, I pray for the skeptics, that You will draw them to Yourself and that one day I will have the privilege of hearing, in every specific detail, how God has moved in their lives!

#MommysHelper

> Guide older women into lives of reverence so they end up as neither gossips nor drunks, but models of goodness. By looking at them, the younger women will know how to love their husbands and children, be virtuous and pure, keep a good house, and be good wives. We don't want anyone looking down on God's Message because of their behavior.

> —Titus 2: 3–5 (MSG)

I met a younger mom at a park one day, and we began talking about parenting and the daily struggles of life in general.

She had a twenty-month old, and when I told her I had four children, she was full of questions: "I just have one, and it's so hard—how do you do it? She continued to express how she was committed to staying at home but she was often frustrated, feeling housebound, and lonely.

I found myself trying to encourage her, telling her that it does indeed go by quickly and that one day she would look back and remember these as some of the best days of her life.

I am amazed at the number of people out in the world who just need an encouraging word. They need to have someone who they can be honest with and express their feelings to. Meeting with that young woman really took me back to her stage of life, and I immediately thought of people in my life who had taken the time to care.

There was an older woman in our neighborhood, by the name of Betty, who would drop in and ask if she could take my two-year-old for a walk so I could get housework done or take a nap while my infant daughter was sleeping. This dear woman, friend, and neighbor would call me up at the spur of the moment and invite us to her backyard for a picnic. Many times the invitations would be the highlight of our day! She would hide eggs in her backyard at Easter time and would have the children come down for a hunt. She gave them art lessons, taking them to the railroad track to first hunt for rocks that they would bring home and use as an canvas for an original painting. She taught most of the neighborhood children to roller skate and to ride bicycles.

She kept me informed of community events that the children would enjoy (this was prior to mom blogs!) and goggled over my children when they were infants. She encouraged me when they were in the more difficult stages and always helped me look forward to each phase with anticipation rather than anxiety.

This dear woman was at that stage of life when her children were no longer at home. She even had grandchildren of her own who lived close by, but she would always include my children in the different activities she planned. Because we were a great distance from my parents, I was so appreciative.

I am so grateful to this woman, among other mentors, for unselfishly walking with me through the different stages of parenting and for reminding me to view my children as individuals and as gifts to enjoy.

Thank You, Lord, for the older women that I know you purposefully placed in my life to be an encouragement and help while I was raising our children. Help me, now an older mom, to look for opportunities to do the same for younger moms.

#PrayerBridge

For in this hope we were saved. But hope that is seen is no hope at all. Who hopes for what they already have? But if we hope for what we do not yet have, we wait for it patiently.

—Romans 8:24–25 (NIV)

I was moving with speed through the house one morning, tackling my daily morning routine, when a close friend who was going through a difficult time came to mind, so I gave her a call.

I just listened as she said, "How do you always know exactly when to call me?" The night before had been a particularly difficult one for her, and the next morning hadn't started out much better. She needed someone to listen.

She explained that she was sitting in the dark with the blinds drawn, which told me she was not in a very good place. Feeling inept at knowing how to encourage her, I just listened and was thinking of how to respond when I saw that one of my four children was trying to phone me. I told my friend that I would call her right back.

My son was in good spirits, and he, too, was on the move with his morning schedule. On that particular morning, this began with driving his three children to school.

He was sharing all that he had to accomplish that day, when he said, "Hey, Mom, we are just coming up to this bridge where I pray with the kids before I drop them off to school."

So encouraged that he was engaging with his children in this way, I quickly said, "Oh, I'll let you go."

Then he responded, "Mom, would you like to pray with us?"

After I got over the shock of what I'd heard come of his mouth, I responded with "Sure!"

After putting me on speaker phone, he asked his children if they had any particular prayer requests. Then he asked me how he could pray for me. I think this was the first time in my life that I found myself speechless. When I hesitated, he said, "How about praying for safety for you and Dad when you go on your trip?"

"That would be great!"

I listened as he prayed that each of his children would have a good day and that they would do well.

When he finished, I gave thanks for my son and his children and for my daughter-in-law, who was working.

He went on to describe how he had been low on gas the other day and had realized his credit card was missing. He had figured out a solution and was sharing how he'd commented to a friend how not too long ago a setback like that would have sent him over the edge and how he would have ranted and raved. I listened and shared in his excitement that he was experiencing some positive changes in his life. We said our goodbyes, and I called my friend back. I shared with her that I had been meant to take that phone call, because I now knew how to encourage her. I told her that there was hope and that the way she was feeling wouldn't last forever. I could tell her because I had been where she was, in what seemed like a hopeless spot. Now God was daily giving me glimpses of a work that he was doing in my son's life. I cried with excitement, and I shared with her the encouraging conversation.

Lord, thank You for friends who walked alongside me on those dark parenting days, who prayed when I had no strength to pray. Those friends got me out of the house when I wanted to wallow in my disappointment and pain. Thank You for leaving the Holy Spirit to be our helper while we struggle on this earth. Even though I can't see You, Your presence is undeniably real and guides your people. Thank You for my restlessness last night, which gave me the opportunity to pray for my children. Thank you for continuously praying for Your children and for never giving up on them!

#RejectedbutChosen

No one will be able to stand against you all the days of your life. As I was with Moses, so I will be with you; I will never leave you nor forsake you.

—Joshua 1:5 (NIV)

Because of the manufacturing nature of the area where I grew up in the Midwest in the early seventies, I was very fortunate and thankful for the opportunity to have some great-paying summer jobs. These helped with my college tuition so I had a minimal amount of debt.

These jobs paid very well for the time, but the nature of the work was beyond boring and repetitive. I remember one particular job so clearly. I was seated at a desk and shown an example of a "perfect" part. If my memory serves me correctly, the part was about the size of a penny. I was told to study the "good" part so I would recognize flaws in the damaged parts. It's the same with counterfeit money: experts study the real bills so that they will recognize the counterfeit. I was then shown some parts with flaws and instructed to trash these. While I tried to be conscientious, I'm sure that a few "perfect" parts were rejected by me, and I'm sure a few "imperfect" parts mistakenly passed through. I looked for rejects all day long.

A tray of hundreds of these parts would be dumped on a desk in front of me, and my job was to sort through them with both hands, as you would sort through old pennies to look for a certain date. I had to do this at quite a fast pace, for as soon as I would get through the pile—or, in most cases, before I would get through the pile—another load would be dumped in front of me! This went on hour after hour, with a half-hour lunch break and maybe two 10-minute breaks. I remember my mind just going elsewhere; I would go into a trance to get me through another eight-hour day.

This job came to mind when my friend was still healing over being rejected by her husband of twenty-five years. She was sharing with me how she was getting along emotionally at that point of her journey. She had come a long way over the last six years, since her husband had walked out on her on the date of their twenty-fifth wedding anniversary.

She explained her feelings. "I have never had anyone in my life who loved me enough to be willing to fight for me!" While she acknowledged that she felt unconditionally loved by her children, she had been rejected by her mom, some of her siblings, and ultimately her husband. Her mom was in a cult, meaning a kind of religious organization that bases its salvation on good works rather than the work of Christ. Because my friend had put her faith in Christ and had become part of mainstream Christianity, she was shunned by her mother, a practice that, however barbaric, still exists.

She was doubting herself, asking me if she was indeed unlovable. I listened and tried to understand and encourage her, but I really felt inadequate to comfort her, since I didn't have a husband who had given up on my marriage. I had felt the pain of rejection from a child, but somehow that was different than the pain of being rejected by the one you'd thought would be your partner for life. I felt as if I were trivializing her pain when I reminded her that God would never reject her. However, I still knew that having a relationship with God was key, so I proceeded to tell her that God loved her with an everlasting love, that He loved her and would never reject her.

At first I felt that my effort to encourage her was ineffectual. However, the next day I was listening to a well-known female speaker encouraging other women who had experienced rejection. She shared the truth that we were chosen in love by God before the creation of the world (Ephesians 1:4–5). Now that's a love that no relationship on this earth can match!

I can't help but think that a time will come when she is totally confident in this love that has been lavished upon her. If she desires it then, God will place a man in her life who will love her the best that he is humanly capable of—but I know that it will pale in comparison to the power of love she has available to her right now!

Dear Lord, please continue to walk with my friend who, though rejected by her earthly husband, will never be rejected by you. Please make her more aware every day of the magnitude of your love so that she will be at peace, resting in that truth.

#VerticallyChallenged

> Dear God, my master, you created earth and sky by your great power … by merely stretching out your arm! There is nothing you can't do.
>
> —Jeremiah 32:17 (MSG)

I have a broom in my garage that is pretty special to me. A friend and neighbor gave it to me, because he likes to tease me about being "vertically challenged." I'm five feet one-and-a-half inches, and I guess he finds that amusing! He had a broken-handled broom in his garage that he was going to throw out, but he gifted it to me, inscribed with my name. I now store it in my garage.

I have never really minded my height, although I have wondered at times what life might look like if I had the opposite perspective. The only time I have ever felt handicapped is when I have tried to get things into kitchen cabinets that are made for "average" heights, the shelves where daily dishes are kept. Often the dishes that live on the top shelves will sit there until I can grab a stool, so I can move several things at once. Even on a stool, I find it difficult to easily put things away. If you are my height, you know the power of hanging onto the edge of a bowl and, while on your tippy toes, raising it vertically and hoping to slide it on top of another bowl without it breaking.

I guess that's why, when I read God's word that said, "Now what I am commanding you today is not too difficult for you or beyond your reach," (Deuteronomy 30: 11 NIV), it spoke to me. That's because I know that most of this world, as I know it, is beyond my reach, and it gives me great hope. He is telling me that while I might have trouble reaching most things, the thing that matters the most, the word of God, is "set" before me, to embrace (sweep up) or dismiss (discount or disregard.)

When Moses asked the Lord if there would be enough food for all the grumbling people, the Lord answered Moses, "Is the Lord's arm too short? Now you will see whether or not what I say will come true for you" (Numbers 11:23 NIV). God then supplied the people with quail.

The Lord offered a lifestyle choice to his people years ago, and the same offer is available today. "I have set before you life and death, blessings and curses. Choose life, so that you and your children may live and that you may love the Lord your God, listen to his voice, and hold fast to him. For the Lord is your life, and he will give you many years in the land he swore to give to your fathers, Abraham, Isaac and Jacob" (Deuteronomy 30:19–20).

Dear Lord, thank You for creating me just the way you did, height and all. While there may be many things that I can't reach because of my height, I am also reminded that I can do nothing apart from you but that with you nothing is impossible!

#WeNeedEachOther

For we are God's masterpieces. He has created us anew in Christ, so that we can do the good things He planned for us long ago.

—Ephesians 2:10 (NLT)

Our four-year-old neighbor boy rang my doorbell one day, asking if my fourteen-year-old son, whom he looked up to, could come out to play. After I explained to his mom that he was at a boater's safety class, we visited, and then I asked if he wanted to ride along with me to pick up my son.

We stopped afterwards to get a summer treat at a fast-food restaurant. While we were waiting in line, a man approached an employee at the counter and asked for a job application. Not thinking anything of it, I went ahead and ordered as my son and his "buddy" sat down. When I glanced up to check on them, I saw them sitting in a booth with the man that I'd seen at the counter. They were helping him to fill out a job application.

The man had handed it to my son and asked him if he would help read it for him. The sight of my son offering his help to this stranger was even more meaningful because my son had struggled with reading himself. To see my son offering this man help, with his little "buddy" watching it all, gave me such a picture of God's love and how He uses His people to help one another.

I was filled with pride as I watched the little buddy observing. I hoped that he was catching a glimpse of true manhood while my son helped another in need.

We truly do need each other. The little neighbor boy needed a friend that day. His mother needed a few minutes to get some things accomplished. The man needed help with his application, and my son and I needed encouragement. I received encouragement that day, when I saw firsthand God's loving hand in all the details of each one of our lives. I saw how He placed all of us in specific locations at specific times to fulfill His greater purpose that day.

Lord, thank You for the incredible way you have of ordering our days and putting people in our lives and in our paths! I thank You for turning an ordinary summer afternoon into anything but ordinary!

CHAPTER 3

GROWING UP WITH CHILDREN

#BabyCanCome

This resurrection life you received from God is not a
timid, grave-tending life. It's adventurously expectant;
greeting God with a childlike "What's next, Papa?"

—Romans 8:15–16 (MSG)

Our daughter and son-in-law were expecting their first child
around Christmastime, and they were busy make plans for the
arrival of their new daughter.

Among some of the first things they purchased in anticipation
were a crib, a changing table, and a rocker. They decided on the color
for the room and planned a mural for the wall.

We knew they were getting excited about setting up the nursery
and had a desire to do crown molding and a chair rail, so when our
daughter asked her daddy if he could help, we planned a trip there.
Some friends of ours offered to go with us to help, so we were able to
knock out the entire room in a weekend. From molding to painting,
hanging curtains and then organizing all the gifts they had been
showered with, we did it all. When the room was complete, our
daughter sat in the rocker and rested. Our son-in-law and daughter
both looked around, seemingly pleased and satisfied that a special
place was now complete to welcome their new baby girl home. They
were excitedly anticipating her arrival!

Shortly after we got home we had our wedding anniversary, and I found myself reminiscing about our own wedding day. I started thinking of my dad and how much I missed him.

The love of a father runs so deep. We all long to be special to our daddies. It was fun to watch my husband help our daughter and son-in-law out in this way. I was reminded of how special I am to my Heavenly Father. Preparing for the arrival of our granddaughter was a reminder of how excited a daddy is as he awaits the arrival of the daughter whom he will love for the rest of his life. It was comforting to think of how even deeper is the love that our Heavenly Father has for us—knowing that He, too, has prepared a room for us and awaits our arrival!

Lord, thank You for being not some distant God but a personal God who loves us and wants us to address you as "Abba—Father!" I am so grateful that, just as a child runs in excitement into its father's arms, we, too, can run to you. I thank You, Lord, that Your word assures us of your everlasting love and that you have prepared a room for us when our time on this earth is complete. As a daddy welcomes his baby girl into this world, you will welcome us into eternity. As the song (by Mercy Me) says, "I Can Only Imagine" what the room you have prepared will look like.

#BrightFuture

Before I shaped you in the womb, I knew all about you. Before you saw the light of day, I had holy plans for you.

—Jeremiah 1:5 (MSG)

Many parents are so excited to share with friends about their high school senior's plans for the future, about his or her scholarships or their acceptance to a particular school. But I bet you can't top my son's dream!

My eighteen-year-old was making plans to flee the nest after the summer of graduation to go to school part time, and mainly to start a business. But what he was really excited about was a trampoline-Velcro room!

He was talking about the plans that he and his buddy were making for after graduation, and his tone quickened with excitement as he told about his idea for a room in the trailer that they hoped to be living in. "We want to have a trampoline in one of the rooms, with Velcro on the ceiling and the walls, and we will have body suits made out of the fuzzy stuff that sticks to Velcro, and we will be able to jump on the trampoline and stick to the walls and ceiling—sweet!"

I'm so glad I was almost fifty when he shared these dreams with me. In earlier years, I would have gone into a long, drawn-out tirade about the impracticality of such a room, not to mention the danger and the cost. But, hey, at that midlife stage, when I was looking for some adventure myself, I said (after I could get control of my laughter), "Cool! Can I come visit and hang out on your ceiling? I remember his brother wanted to be a trash man in New York City about this stage of his senior year, because he had heard that they got paid a lot and it would be a great way to tour the city!

"What is your son doing next year?" I was asked.

"Oh, my boy is totally focusing on his future. He is moving up north, because the hunting and fishing are good, and the cost of living is cheaper, and the schools are cheaper and easier to get into, and he's going to have his very own Velcro-lined room in his trailer, where he can rest on the ceiling or walls after a hard day at his asphalt job."

You know, I don't think one out of our four children have fit into my expectations about what their senior year would be like. Expectations have gotten me in trouble my entire life.

Dear Lord, forgive me for getting caught up in what our culture views as success. Thanks for reminding me that this child that You have loaned to us and the child that you gave life to—not once, not twice, but three times—is secure in your mighty hands, which are stronger than the toughest Velcro. Whatever the future holds, You always have and always will continue to be the bond that is stronger than any man-made Velcro. You will let him and his mom rest in You, and no matter what he decides to do, it will be a "bright future."

#CalltheDoc

A happy heart makes the face cheerful, but heartache crushes the spirit.

—Proverbs 15:13 (NIV)

Adolescence brings many changes. One of the changes that came to haunt one of our three sons was a swollen "breast." The medical term is gynecomastia.

When you are a fifteen-year-old male, it just isn't cool to have a breast at all. Our son, fortunately, had a real sense of humor about it and would, without prompting, show it to anyone and everyone who visited our home! Knowing that humor can be a cover-up for pain, we tried to be sensitive to his situation and made the appointment with a doctor to appease him and assure him that this wouldn't be with him for a lifetime. The doctor assured us that it was, indeed, very common and that it would certainly go away eventually.

Months later, it was still there and was still bothering him a lot. We encouraged him to be patient and assured him that God cared about even this situation. Thus we continued as a family to pray for this breast, which was in itself humorous! After weeks of doubting whether God was hearing his prayers, he insisted that we make another doctor's appointment to see what could be done about this situation.

He told all his neighborhood friends that that was the day when he would finally find a solution to his problem. We arrived at the pediatrician's office; yes, he wasn't old enough to make the transition to a family doc yet. I picked up a pamphlet in the office, and while we waited we read about changes during adolescence. We laughed because they had swollen breasts listed under changes in girls but not under changes in boys. When the doctor came into the room, my son explained the situation to her, and she began to examine him.

She confirmed that the condition was indeed normal, especially with a big growth spurt as he had experienced, and that it would most certainly go away. He listened and was polite until we got out of the office, and then Mom had to endure the brunt of his anger. "That stupid doctor! What does she know? Why doesn't she just cut the thing out? Did you see her feeling me? I think she was enjoying it. I can't take it anymore." I listened and tried to encourage him, telling him that it was just a matter of time.

As we were pulling out of the parking lot, a Muskogee duck swooped in front of our car and almost hit our windshield. My son must have seen this as an opportunity to release his tension without Mom getting mad; he yelled out, "That stupid duck!" We laughed until we cried as we both felt the release of tension and realized that humor would get us through this troubling time!

Lord, thank You for creating us with the ability to laugh. It has really helped us get through some tough times.

#DontWorryBeHappy

Give your entire attention to what God is doing right now, and don't get worked up about what may or may not happen tomorrow. God will help you deal with whatever hard things come up when the time comes.

—Matthew 6:34 (MSG)

I was finally getting out of the house to head for the grocery store, after a full day of cleaning and organizing a baby shower for my neighbor.

As I was backing out of my driveway, I noticed that my fuel light was on, so I headed to the closest gas station. On the way, I noticed my nineteen-year-old son's car parked on the side of the road, and I saw him looking under the back of a pickup. I didn't think much of it. He was probably helping a friend with some car trouble, I guessed, so I went ahead and got my gas. I thought I'd look and see if he was still there after I was finished.

As I headed back down the road, I saw my son walking toward me, toward the gas station, so I stopped. He informed me that he had been checking out the fella's vehicle because he had rear-ended him. Instead of asking whether he was okay, I shook my head and said, "Your insurance will skyrocket!"

He patiently said, "I know, Mom. Could you please just call Dad and have him "Nextel" me, so that I can find my phone, so I can call the police?"

"What do you mean, 'so you can find it'?"

"Mom, it flew out of the car or something when I hit him."

I said okay and headed home. After I had called my husband, I headed for the grocery.

As I passed them, I saw that the police had arrived and were talking with both of them. It felt as weird as a mom to drive on by, knowing there was nothing I could do now but pray. "Lord, you know my son, and You know how hard he is working and how discouraged he is with circumstances that he is going through. I know a ticket would be yet another financial setback right now, but You know him better than I do. You know his heart, and You know whether a ticket would be the best thing for him, so I'm trusting You to work in this situation." I went on to the grocery store, shopped, prayed, and tried to trust.

A young man was helping me to the car with my cartload of groceries, and I asked him whether he was out of school. "Oh yes, ma'am. I graduated two years ago." I told him I'd thought that he was in his early twenties, that I had a son that age. He continued, "I bet your son isn't engaged and has a baby on the way!"

I told him no, that was true, but that I had another son who was twenty-four who had started his family around twenty-one. I asked him whether he loved the girl, and he said, "More than anything." I asked if he was going to marry her, and he said yes. I asked if his parents were supportive. He shared that he didn't really know if the girl's parents were, that he was hoping, but that his mom was an alcoholic, and he wasn't really close to her. He didn't mention anything about his dad.

I told him I was sorry and shared a favorite Bible verse: "Trust in the Lord with all your heart and lean not on your own understanding; in all your ways submit to Him and He will make your paths straight" (Proverbs 3:5 NIV). He shared a favorite Bible verse of his, and I thanked him as we smiled at each other, encouraged by our "chance" meeting.

When I arrived home, I discovered that the officer hadn't written a ticket because our son had agreed to replace the man's bumper. That night our son said, "Man, I was driving down the interstate and thinking, *It has been a long time since I had an accident, thank You, God,* and then *bam!*" My husband and I looked at each other and silently chuckled, and then his dad told him that he needed to start listening to that voice in his head, that just possibly the Holy Spirit had been giving him a personal warning to stay alert and pay attention.

I had finished up the dinner dishes and was ready to put my feet up and relax a bit, when my son yelled, "Mom, the toilets are gurgling; they are plugged up." My husband said we needed to get a septic guy out the next day, to pump us out before the party that weekend. *Goodnight everyone. I'll make the call tomorrow.*

The next day I e-mailed my eldest son at work, telling him what had happened with his brother. He returned this e-mail as I awaited the arrival of the "honey dipper." His reply was, "Poor kid. I kind of feel bad for him; he has had a lot of stuff happen to him. But now that I think about it, it happens to all of us. He is going through a rough part of life; he just needs to figure stuff out. We will have to be patient; young men can stay lost for a long time. I know I was and still to this day have to refocus weekly and sometimes daily. We will pray for you and Dad and your abilities to deal with him."

Wow! Thank You, Lord, for the encouragement from my son, who at one point drove us so crazy that my husband and I didn't think we'd live through it! Thanks for reminding me that there is always hope!

#GetaJob

> Too much talk leads to sin. Be sensible and keep your mouth shut.
>
> —Proverbs 1:13 (NLT)

When my eldest child was a mouthy, know-it-all teen and mad at me for trying to hold him accountable, he actually said just that!

A dear friend who has been through many trials of her own has a favorite saying, "Life has a way of biting you in the rear end!" In my son's case, this came to pass when he found himself, in his first year of marriage, staying home as a full-time "house husband" while his new bride finished up her military duty.

I was very proud of myself for listening to his struggles of fatherhood in this role as mother without uttering the words "I told you so." Well, okay, I confess. I didn't say those exact words, but I did say, "Do you remember when you said to me, 'Mom, why don't you get a "real job"?'" I'm sorry—I'm only human!

I listened as he said, "Mom, she is so strong; she is holding her head up already!" I listened as he said, "She sat up for a few seconds!" I listened as he said, "She is pulling herself up." I listened as he said, "She is saying Mama, but not Dada." I listened as he said, "I taught her to say Papa!" I listened as he said she would smile at him when he looked sternly at her and told her not to touch the hot stove or to get into the garbage. I listened as he said he would try to comfort her afterward to affirm his love, and she would push him away. I listened as he said he would feel kind of bad when his wife came home and the baby was so glad to see her, after he had cared for her every need all day. I listened as he said, "I have to get out of here!" I listened as he said, "Mom, I think she is going to be so smart!" I listened as he said, "Mom, she has her first tooth!" I sympathized as he said he was upset about gaining twenty pounds. I listened as he said, "She is taking her first steps!" I laughed as he declared he would never sit his child in front of the television. I laughed as he said that a stupid purple dinosaur had become his best friend and that this dinosaur must be demonic because of the hold it had over children.

I prayed that Jesus would draw my son unto Him. I prayed that God would give him strength to do this job he had been called to. I prayed that he would grow to be a husband who loved his wife as Christ loved the church. I prayed that his wife would be drawn to Christ and that she would love him unconditionally. I prayed that they both would be committed to their marriage vows. I prayed that they would look to God to help them through the struggles of the daily routine of parenting. I prayed that Jesus, not a purple dinosaur, would soon become his "bestest" friend.

I didn't say, "Why you don't get a 'real job'?" I didn't have to. God has called him.

Thank You, Lord, for enabling me to hold my tongue and for the opportunity to share my son's parental excitement. Thank You for the joy I hear in his voice today in this God-given calling.

#GoodNews

Like a cool drink of water when you're worn out and weary is a letter from a long-lost friend.

—Proverbs 25:25 (MSG)

I couldn't have said it better. There is nothing quite as encouraging as good news, especially if you are a mom and the news involves your child, no matter what his or her age.

Maybe it's because, as we age, we come to know the strengths and weaknesses of our children so well. We may have experienced near-empty hope meters for so long that when a door opens we know there is no other explanation than that God is at work!

One of "My Three Sons," in my eyes, had been floundering a bit in life. He was out on his own, but he didn't appear to be focusing on his future. I should qualify that: I mean a future that I thought would result in a life filled with peace and positive consequences. Because this particular son had been brought through so much, including two near-death experiences, I found it much easier to "let go." I had seen God, literally, spare his life twice, with a near-drowning at eleven months and a life-threatening auto accident when he was a teen. I knew that if he had been brought through these serious, life-threatening situations and lived, then God had decided it wasn't his time to leave this earth. God was certainly capable of moving in his life in what seemed, by comparison, less critical areas.

This son had called and said that a high school friend had recommended him for a job. This son had always loved the water and fishing—not necessarily more than the other two did, but he loved it so much that he wanted to make his living at it. The job was as a deckhand on a tugboat. I just knew that God had answered my prayers by plucking him right out of his present situation and moving him to another continent!

I bought a map and hung it so we could chart his course. On one particular run, we watched the news intently, as I knew he was in the Caribbean, dodging hurricanes that were forming all around him!

He had been gone for several days when that first e-mail came. I jumped for joy when I saw his name in my mailbox. I couldn't click that mail open quickly enough!

As I read about this new adventure of his, I was reminded that

God sees us as his children. He is just as excited when we contact Him to share what's going on in our lives as we as parents are to hear from our children. We are so fickle. We *so* quickly forget how God has moved in our own lives and in the lives of our children. When our circumstances reflect the outcome we like, we are happy with God, but when we don't like our circumstances, we question whether He is even around or if He cares.

Thankfully, we can be encouraged by knowing that we aren't the first to feel this way. God has left us many stories to show us His faithfulness in spite of the doubts of His people. When God had just rebuked the Red Sea to save His people, then they believed His promises and sang His praise. Can you imagine seeing the sea split in half? You'd think if you had witnessed such a miracle that you would no longer be skeptical, but evidence of our stubbornness exists. "After our parents left Egypt, they took your wonders for granted, forgot your great and wonderful love. They were barely beyond the Red Sea when they defied the High God ... the very place he saved them! ... the place he revealed his amazing power! He rebuked the Red Sea so that it dried up on the spot ... he paraded them right through! No one so much as got wet feet! He saved them from a life of oppression, pried them loose from the grip of the enemy. Then the waters flowed back on their oppressors; there wasn't a single survivor. Then they believed his words were true and broke out in songs of praise." But it wasn't long before they forgot the whole thing and wouldn't wait to be told what to do. They only cared about pleasing themselves in that desert and provoked God with their insistent demands. He gave them exactly what they asked for. But along with it they got empty hearts. They soon forgot what He had done and did not wait for his counsel. "Many times He delivered them, but they were bent on rebellion and they wasted away in their sin and it continues. ... But he took note of their distress when he heard their cry; for their sake he remembered his covenant and out of His great love he relented" (Psalm 106 MSG).

Lord, forgive me and Your people for doubting Your goodness

and for so quickly forgetting the incredible ways You have worked in our lives and the lives of our children. Help me to continue to trust and wait in expectation for all that You have planned for our lives and the lives of our children and the promised life after this life. "This confidence is like a strong and trustworthy anchor for our souls" (Hebrews 6:19).

#GreatestGift

For it is by grace you have been saved, through faith and this not from yourselves, it is the gift of God— not by works, so that no one can boast.

—Ephesians 2:8–9 (NIV)

We were celebrating an early Christmas with our oldest son and daughter-in-law and their two toddlers before they headed up north to be with her family. We couldn't wait for the treasure hunt we had planned. In it they would search for clues that would be tropic based and would ultimately take them to a red stocking that held the details of their first cruise together!

Our youngest son videotaped, and my husband and I each toted one of the grandchildren, so they could watch their parents discover presents throughout the yard.

It was fun following them as they went from clue to clue with visions of "sugar plums" dancing in their heads: suntan lotion, beach towel, etc. When they got to the final clue and pulled the gift from the stocking that was all hung with care, the tears started to flow from the receivers of the gift as well as the givers.

As we talked about the trip in excitement, our daughter-in-law said that they didn't deserve the trip. She said there were others who were "better" and more deserving. I'm not sure why she said that, but I think she meant that she was humbled by the gift. My husband and

I remembered how hard it had been with toddlers and how much we'd enjoyed those times when we could be together away from the children. The times had been few, but they were precious. And then I thought again of what she'd said. She was right. None of us deserve anything, and that is exactly what this annual exchange of gifts is all about.

Her spirit had perfectly captured what the Christmas season should mean. All of us fall short and deserve nothing but God's wrath, but the greatest gift ever given was the birth of Jesus. I often wonder why God came in the form of a child, rather than a full-grown king, especially when that is what God's people were expecting. I don't have all the answers, but I do know that He became a baby and experienced life through to adulthood. That way He could make the ultimate sacrifice of dying so that I and everyone else who accepts his deity could be assured of life unending. We are better able to love our children because we have walked in their shoes. Maybe He wanted to experience all the challenges we face as humans so He could better understand and love us. I think that's more than a maybe.

Isaiah prophesied thousands of years before the birth of Christ that the Lord would choose a sign. "Look! The virgin will conceive a child! She will give birth to a son and will call him Immanuel … God is with us" (Isaiah 7:14). It was out of love for our children that we wanted to give them this gift that we thought they would enjoy.

Thank you, Jesus, for teaching us how to love our children by Your perfect example of sacrificial love. Thanks for loving me, Your child, so much that You were born and died and drew me to Yourself. That way I could accept your precious gift of eternal life, which I didn't deserve! In a world of performance, it is difficult for us to accept a gift with no strings attached. Your word said that it is simple enough for a child to understand. That's it! When we come to this understanding we, the receiver, can only shed tears of joy when we glimpse the depth of Your love for us. Happy birthday, Jesus!

#HomeAllDay

Whoever fears the Lord has a secure fortress, and
for their children it will be a refuge.

—Proverbs 14:26 (NIV)

I found myself floundering shortly after that New Year,
wondering how I would spend my time. I had been organizing and
trying to clean out, but because I am so people oriented, I can only
spend so many days home alone without going stir crazy.

I talked to my husband about the possibility of going back to
work, but I had committed to taking my mom, who had been recently
widowed, on a couple of trips that would be difficult if I had a full-time
job. I also had a lifelong friend coming for a visit, and I was having fun
setting up a guest room—the first time in thirty-five years of marriage
that I had an official guest room! I had shared as my prayer request at my
women's Bible study that I would appreciate some direction for this stage
of my life. I needed help to figure out what my new calling would be.

After carrying out my morning routine, I decided to get out
the material that I had already written and see whether I could get
inspired to work on completing my devotional book, which my
husband had been encouraging me for years to finish. I explained to
him that I was out of material since the children were gone and that
he would have to help provide me with new material. A friend called
as I was trying to figure out my morning, a new empty nester herself,
and she encouraged me to write about this post-children stage.

As I started to work, the phone rang, and it was our newly
married daughter. She was on her way to work and was sharing her
morning with me. She informed me that her husband had witnessed
one of her "meltdowns," meaning an overreaction to the pressures
of life, and that they had been able to laugh about it together. I told
her about what I was trying to accomplish, and she encouraged me
to get a small "notebook" computer to make it easier.

As I got back to the task at hand, the phone rang again, and this time it was my youngest son, calling from North Carolina. While he was discouraged with a truck that kept breaking down, I heard a calmness in his voice that I had never heard before. He told me about a church he had been visiting and how the messages there were, amazingly, about some of the very questions he and a friend had been discussing.

Wow, do I miss him! But it is so neat to see him growing in his faith!

While I'd been talking to him, my cell phone had rung, so after I hung up, I checked my messages. I saw that it was my second-eldest son, who was in Louisiana. He was the one who worked on a tug, and he let me know that their plans might have changed, that with the devastation in Haiti they would be headed there with a barge full of supplies.

Lord, thank You for your direction today. I didn't want to stay home, but it was your plan for me to stay home today. If I had been running, I would have missed the encouragement of talking and catching up with three of the children You loaned to me! I guess it really is true that our children still need us and that I will never be done being a mother. I will continue to pursue what You are calling me to daily and wait expectantly to see where you lead!

#NoRest

We also pray that you will be strengthened with all his glorious power so you will have all the endurance and patience you need. May you be filled with joy, always thanking the Father. He has enabled you to share in the inheritance that belongs to his people, who live in the light.

—Colossians 1:11 (NLT)

Do you ever feel as if you are starting to be able to enjoy life a little bit when—*bam!*—something comes up that just leaves you feeling ill in the pit of your stomach?

My husband and I had enjoyed a nice productive Saturday working on a room addition, with the help of our youngest son. We were unwinding after eating dinner and my husband, hoping for some relief for his tired muscles, decided to go soak in the tub. Our son had headed to the mall to meet a friend, so we thought. Then the phone rang.

It was the local police, asking if anyone in our household owned a vehicle with a license tag number of such and such. "Yes, sir, that is the tag number of our son. Is everything okay?"

"Well, your son was in a vehicle with another kid, and they were on private church property, driving recklessly around a man who was on a tractor grading the drive, and doing donuts in the parking lot. Will you please tell your son not to set foot on this property again?"

"Yes, sir, I will do more than that." So much for a nice, relaxing evening. I couldn't wait to get hold of the kid and the keys. I should have been thankful that just a warning was being given, but once I learned that everything was really okay, I was ready to strangle him. I never thought I'd be telling one of my sons to stay away from church!

After he finally got home, we read him the riot act and took his keys away for at least a month. We went to bed tired and discouraged, only to wake up at 3 a.m. to the realization that our nineteen-year-old wasn't home yet. We phoned him and found that we had awakened him. He had gone down to visit his girlfriend at college and fallen asleep. A parent desires to believe the best, but you really have no clue about the decisions they are making. When he walks in the door, you're thankful he made it home alive, but you're ready to strangle him for keeping you awake and concerned.

The next day I had the discussion with him about making good decisions in the sexual area and reminded him how much trouble he was having getting financially independent. I pointed out that bringing a child into the world right now would give him a new view of financially strapped. It would also complicate his girlfriend's life, as she was working toward a nursing degree.

I am so ready for these kids to be on their own and to live with their own consequences. I'm tired of being the parent who is called when they make stupid decisions. I'm tired of trying to know how much to help and when helping them is too much.

Lord, please give us patience to finish this job of parenting these children that You have entrusted to our care. Lord, help us to remember that Your word tells us they are a blessing and a gift, when right now they feel like just the opposite. Lord, help us to love them as You love us, unconditionally, and when we do mess up in the way that we parent, let that point them to You who, unlike us, are able to love them perfectly.

#NotGettingEasier

Don't you see that children are God's best gift? The fruit of the womb his generous legacy? Like a warrior's fistful of arrows are the children of a vigorous youth. Oh, how blessed are you parents, with your quiver full of children! Your enemies don't stand a chance against you; you'll sweep them right off your doorstep.

—Psalm 127:3–5 (MSG)

Once again I found myself preparing to let one of my children go. I'd thought that after I had done it twice it would get easier, but I have learned that a painful passage cannot be avoided with the releasing of each child.

As unique as each child was, so was their flight from the nest. This time I was in the process of releasing our third child, our second son. It was clear that it was time. I find it interesting that each time there are circumstances that I think will make it easier, circumstances that at first make it obvious to me that it *is* time. This time it was his irresponsibility in leaving food out to spoil. Our house was running on generators after a hurricane, and food was not only at a premium cost but also scarce. It was clearly time for him to purchase his own food and to be responsible for taking care of it as well. He was twenty years old and had just gone back to work after a four-month recovery from a serious accident. I had been helping care for him and assisting him with all the necessary paperwork that such an accident generates. I was thankful for that time we'd had together, but in my heart I knew that this baby bird needed a little push. My head told me that it was time, the dirty clothes thrown all over his room told me it was time, but my heart told me that it was going to hurt. I'm always left surprised that even though the time has come, the process isn't any less painful. I'm thankful for the signs that the timing is right, though, for somehow it eases the pain.

The heart is a complex organ. The only thing I can think of to describe the impending process is the countdown of the ball drop in New York City to welcome in the New Year. I know it is coming, time is marching on, but I'm leaving not only the memories of one year but of twenty years. As with each year, I reflect on the good times, the bad times, and my hope for the future. I feel the emotion of the past twenty years, and the emotion is like lava in a volcano, ready to spew. Experience tells me that I will weep convulsively for at least a day and then I will be okay. I know it is coming, and I know I will survive.

I believed that with this son in particular it would be easier, because I'd had to release him several times throughout his life. I'd had to release him when he was eleven months old, as he nearly drowned in a backyard swimming pool. I'd had to release him to doctors when he was four, to rebuild his elbow after a fall from a slide at a park. I'd had to watch him go through lots of pain and rehabilitation after he was ejected from a vehicle on the interstate. He had survived all this, so you'd think that I would have had the assurance that my heavenly Father could protect him, as He had already done numerous times. But it was nonetheless difficult.

Lord, thank You for the nineteen years we have had with this child, nineteen more than we thought we would ever get to have. I'm thankful for those years that I thought I would never see when we nearly lost him to a near-drowning in our backyard pool. I am thankful for every minute, and every day, and every extra year You gave us with him. Thank You for entrusting us with his care and for loving him with a love even greater than ours.

#Payback

When I was an infant at my mother's breast, I gurgled and cooed like any infant. When I grew up, I left those infant ways for good. We don't yet see things clearly. We're squinting in a fog, peering through a mist. But it won't be long before the weather clears and the sun shines bright! We'll see it all then, see it all as clearly as God sees us, knowing him directly just as he knows us! But for right now, until that completeness, we have three things to do to lead us toward that consummation. Trust steadily in God, hope unswervingly, love extravagantly. And the best of the three is love.

—1Corinthians 13:11 (MSG)

When I hit forty-seven, I was forced into a new exercise regime. This was in an effort to get unnecessary weight off, in hopes of lowering my cholesterol. During this period my husband was laid up with a bum foot, after a splinter had become lodged in the pad of his foot. So for a couple of weeks I lost the exercise partner I'd had.

Desperate to continue with my regime, I asked my youngest son, who was then fifteen, to "ple-e-e-ease" take a country-mile ride with me on our tandem. He agreed only when I said, "Do it or its bedtime." I had no idea I was in for the ride of a lifetime.

I quickly came to the conclusion that, because of the ultimatum, he was seeking revenge. After we mounted the bike and started off, he took me straight for the first dip, through a neighbor's yard. After I screamed, "No, stay on the road!" he pulled it back onto the road and headed for the next gully. He yelled, "Keep pedaling, Mom!" He continued with his antics, letting go of the handlebars while saying, "Watch this, Ma—no hands!"

He then swerved back and forth and looked for sand in the road or gravel in a driveway, anything to get me riled! At one point he jumped off the bike when he heard rustling in the nearby woods. He wanted to see whether it was a hog that he had been stalking. Back on, we headed down a busy street to finish off our block. I kept leaning to the left, hoping not to rake my right side against the light poles that were flying by, while he kept commenting at all the people who were staring at us as they went by in cars. He was meanwhile observing how "dumb" he looked riding this bike with his mom. Then he started resting his feet on his handlebars and yelling, "You work it, Mom," making me pedal the rest of the way home by myself. We careened into the driveway, me breathing a sigh of relief and him laughing and saying, "Man, I hope I'm not such a scaredy-cat when I'm your age!"

Lord, being a mom of teens can be quite challenging. Help me to trust and hope and, above all, love as You love.

#RoleReversal

Thank God! Once you were slaves of sin, but now you wholeheartedly obey this teaching we have given you. Now you are free from your slavery to sin, and you have become slaves to righteous living.

—Romans 6:18 (NLT)

I have justified my disdain for exercising for the sake of exercise with the Bible verse found in 1 Timothy 4:8 (NIV): "For physical training is of some value, but godliness has value for all things, holding promise for both the present life and the life to come."

Then I turned fifty and failed the dreaded cholesterol test. In an effort to encourage me, my daughter bought me a membership to a "fun" gym where you exercise to music. She knew me well enough to know that if it resembled dancing more than exercise I might stick to it.

While I was overwhelmed with her thoughtfulness, generosity, and concern, I still had to force myself to get dressed in the appropriate clothing, get in my car, and walk into the place, knowing that a half hour later I'd be walking out, dragging tail and perspiring like a dog.

My daughter was home recently for a visit and asked me to take a three-mile speed walk with her. My response was, "Three miles? Don't you think, since I am just starting out, that I should only do a mile?"

To this she replied, "Mom, you easily walk three miles when you're shopping; it is just that you don't think you can do it—or is it?"

My response was, "I know I can, I just don't want to!" I knew I had been exposed, and there was no turning back. I did survive the walk.

I suddenly realized that our relationship had changed. Maybe I had shortchanged this motherhood calling too quickly. My daughter, who just a few short years ago had seen me as nothing but an annoyance, was now wanting to be around me and wanting to encourage me! I also recalled that as I had pushed her to overcome her fears, she was now doing the same for me.

She called today and asked me what I was doing. I told her that I been exercising and that I had finally found my pulse, which caused her to break out in laughter. "You didn't have one, Mom?"

She went on to share her day with me. My daughter is a hairstylist, and she had been asked by a client to be the entertainment at her thirteen-year-old daughter's luau birthday party. She would be giving the girls "updos."

The mom had recently gone through a separation from her husband, who had allegedly been involved in some illegal activity that she was unaware of. Now her mother was suffering with cancer, so she was going to be moving closer to her parents. My daughter had found some butterfly necklaces to give to the girls, along with a mug that read "Hope" for the mom as a going-away present. She asked me if I knew of any good Bible verses to go with the butterfly necklaces. Trying to maintain my composure, I asked her, "What about the verse that was on the shirt you bought at the Women of Faith conference we went to?" That verse was, "You have set my heart free" (Psalm 119:32).

This time, joy oozed out of my pores as I heard my daughter thinking of ways to serve and encourage others, out of gratitude for her heart being set free. I really did find my pulse today.

Lord, thank You giving me a glimpse of how You are working in my daughter's life and giving her the desire to use the gifts You have given her to serve and encourage others!

#StupidMove

First pride, then the crash … the better the ego, the harder the fall.

—Proverbs 16:18 (MSG)

It was a hot Fourth of July weekend, and my husband and I had worked out in the hot South Florida sun all day. We were ready to take a break.

One of our sons was recovering from a car accident and had gone for a river ride in our neighbor's pontoon boat with a girl he was seeing. His older brother had joined them with our three-year-old granddaughter.

We decided to take a break and meet up with them in the river. We took our little john boat with a twenty-five-horse motor, which I later learned was a bit big for the size of the boat. We putted along the river, and when we got to the T where we could see the boys, my husband thought it would be fun to play a bit. He opened up the motor to create a wake, so the pontoon would begin rocking. I was in the front right side of the boat, hanging onto the side, and as he revved the motor it took every bit of my strength to hold onto the side of the boat to avoid falling out.

I started to become angry, as I was really uncomfortable from the extreme angle I was at. I turned around to express my outrage—only to discover that he was no longer in the boat himself! My anger turned to survival mode when I saw that the boat was now taking on water. Everyone around me was yelling to get to the front of the boat to prevent it from sinking, which I quickly did.

My husband had no visible injuries, but he did sustain some fractured ribs, which he had to live with for several weeks. He was humbled but able to laugh—not without discomfort—when we heard that our granddaughter, upon seeing her grandpa fly out of the boat, had responded with, "Silly Grandpa!"

Lord, thank You for Your protection of my husband and myself today. Grandpa was acting silly today, but the outcome could have been much worse. We thank You for our well-being tonight.

#TeenbehindWheel

But when I am afraid, I will put my trust in you. I praise God, so why should I be afraid? What can mere mortals do to me?

—Psalm 56:3–4 (NLT)

Driver's license. A rite of passage for that young person on the outskirts of the adult world.

We had survived the permit training period. Despite all of my intentions of handling that period differently than my own parents had, I still wasn't able to resist the temptation to ask my son how he expected to drive responsibly with that radio blaring and to draw his attention to the heavy foot he seemed to have inherited.

I was really depressed when I found my knuckles turning purple from grasping the armrest so tightly. I justified my behavior with the fact that I was teaching my son in a full-sized van rather than the VW beetle that my dad had taught me on. I had every reason to be overly cautious. This was a lot of vehicle for a "boy" to handle. We had delayed letting him take his driver's test for his regular license, hoping to observe some signs of maturity. When we didn't see these, we decided to let him get what he so desperately wanted. We were thinking that maybe if we gave him some responsibility he would have a desire to work on the maturity.

Our memories are funny things. I can't remember names very well, along with a lot of other things, but I remember the day I took my driver's test as if it were yesterday.

Now, as I peered around the building where the drivers' tests were being given and watched my son back out of the parking space with the instructor in the seat next to him, I had butterflies all over again. I noticed I wasn't the only one reminiscing. A man whom I'd seen walking up to the building with his son was watching him back out also, and he commented to me that he also remembered "that day" quite vividly.

On the way to the license bureau, a song had come on the radio about watching your little boy grow up and hearing him say to his father: "Dad, I want to be just like you." The song continued with the father praying over his child while he was asleep. "Father, I want to be just like you" (I Want to Be Just Like You, by Craig & Dean Phillips).

It took me back to this now-sixteen-year-old's toddler days, and the thought of him now driving me on this interstate was overwhelming. How could it have gone by so fast? How could I let go, trust him, and trust God to take care of my baby?

As the music faded, I wiped my tears away so my son wouldn't notice. He didn't need me to be sentimental at this moment. I regained my composure and prepped him with what he might expect on the test.

As I arrived home and went to write about my experience of letting go, feeling that I had done just that, the phone rang. It was my husband, letting me know that I had almost been made a widow. A semi-truck that he was following had lost a brake drum, and it had shot through my husband's truck windshield like a bullet. Fortunately, he had dodged it, and although he had shattered glass all over him, he was unharmed. Once again I was reminded that God has things under control. He did choose to protect my husband from being killed that day. Had he been killed, He would have helped me work through that as well.

Okay, Lord, now that he has his driver's license, I turn him over to You. I turn his strengths, his weaknesses, his will, and his life over to you. We have taught him what we know and believe to be truth. I pray that You will reveal Yourself to him.

The son I wrote about is now thirty-seven and has three children of his own. I was just recently reminded of what a difficult milestone this is for moms as I was introduced to a young man who was about to get his license. As I was talking to the young man's parents, I noticed the mom welling up with tears. "Where did the time go?" she asked. "It went so fast." The son walked away, embarrassed by his mom's display of emotion. I told her that I understood and knew she would be okay. I wished I could take away her worries and concerns, but I can't. This is her journey, but she doesn't have to walk it alone.

#ThisisTough

Don't you see that children are God's best gift? The
fruit of the womb his generous legacy?

—Psalm 127:3 (MSG)

The day has arrived where our daughter is venturing out on her
own. She is packing up her room so that we can move her into her
new apartment. She will be working full time and going to school
part time.

I knew the day would arrive, but I'm finding myself totally
unprepared. As I was going about my morning routine, picking
up and putting things away, I walked into her room to see how the
packing was going. The stillness, the emptiness, things I thought
would never come, have arrived. Now that the time is here, it is
haunting me.

My mind wanders back to the grandmother in the grocery
store who, while doting on my daughter sitting in the grocery cart,
told me to enjoy her, because they grow so quickly. I thought the
woman was crazy; each day seemed so long at the time, in the midst
of raising four little children. But she was right. I don't know where
the last twenty years have gone.

I know that life is always changing, but the realization that the
kids are getting older means that I am getting older as well. I am
now the older generation, and our daughter is entering society as a
new adult.

I know it is the normal course of events, but why does it have to
be so painful at this moment? Why is her life passing through my
mind like the reruns of a movie? Will the heartache go away? Will
I move on? What will my life look like?

Yes, I have two teens at home to raise still, but that doesn't
seem to ease the pain that I'm feeling. Is it because she is my only
daughter? Are these tears that I can't stop just part of the normal

process of letting her go? Is this the cutting of the apron strings? It feels more like the tearing out of my heart.

If I know it is time, and I know that she is leaving on good terms, then why is it so painful? Why am I fighting the tears? I've heard it said that God created tears for a purpose, that they are healing. I guess I just need to go through this process of grieving as my daughter moves out into the great big world. I love you. I wouldn't even think of stopping you from going. I will try to hide my sadness so that it won't make this more difficult for you. I will put on my brave front as we drive away. Thanks for all the joy you've brought into our lives. Thanks for being an obedient daughter. Thanks for being my little helper and the servant that you have been and are now. I think the time has arrived when you are no longer just my daughter but also my friend, and I look forward to the times that we will share as friends.

Love, Mom

Dear Lord, thank You for every minute we have been able to share with our daughter. She has been such a joy, and we will miss her. But we gave her to You from the beginning and are reminded in a huge way today that she really belongs to You and not to us. Thank You for the privilege of being a part of her life for these past twenty years. We turn her over to Your perfect care.

#WorthyofPraise

Therefore, let us offer through Jesus a continual sacrifice of praise to God, proclaiming our allegiance to his name. And don't forget to do good and to share with those in need. These are the sacrifices that please God.

—Hebrews 13:15–16 (NLT)

The first Mother's Day since my brother and sister-in-law lost their thirteen-year-old son was approaching, and I knew it would be a difficult day.

My husband and I had been praying that God would comfort them and hold them as only He is capable of.

My sister-in-law had been invited to a retreat for mothers who have lost children, and we prayed that she would be encouraged in just the way she needed.

She really hadn't wanted to go, but circumstances and work schedules worked out and doors that had been closed were opening. This indicated to her that God really did desire for her to be there. She listened and made plans to go, in spite of her feelings.

She texted me soon afterwards and told me that she would be calling to share with me how God had moved in her life.

She talked about intentional praise. She said she had cried out to God, "I don't understand why! I know You didn't cause it, but You could have stopped it." She explained that her focus had changed from *why* to *who* God was, and she concluded that He was worthy of praise, in spite of her circumstances. She knew this to be true, but now she decided to act upon it, to praise God in spite of the horrific circumstances she had lived through as a mother. She had carried her precious child for nine months, and now she had been grieving for nine months. She decided to begin with intentional praise.

I listened, and I explained to her that she was encouraging me as she shared the conclusion she had come to. I told her that I had reached a similar conclusion concerning a circumstance with one of my children. She had lost a child due to a physical death, but I was also feeling a sense of loss. I hadn't lost a child to a physical death, but I had experienced separation, which felt similar to a death experience. I was amazed when she, knowing the situation, said, "That has to be even harder!"

Unable to imagine what she must have endured, that caught me off guard. I was so proud of her for plodding through the months one day at a time, with her faith intact. I then realized that we had both been grieving but holding onto hope. She had the assurance that she would one day see her son again in heaven. I was holding onto the hope that my child's heart would be changed. At that moment God allowed us to connect by each understanding in a small way the pain that the other was experiencing. Our circumstances were very different, but we were both holding onto the giver of hope. Sister-in-law by my brother's choice, sisters in Christ, by God's great design!

I later arrived home from visiting my own mother, and as I was sitting down to relax, I got a call from my sister-in-law. Her voice was upbeat, as I hadn't heard it since the tragedy! One of her sons, my nephew, had invited her to a Phil Wickham concert for Mother's Day. One of Phil's songs, "Heaven Song," had been the favorite song of my nephew. This particular son had been struggling as well with the loss of his youngest brother and had been unmotivated with life in general, partly because of his age and most recently because of his grief. My sister-in-law went on, "We went to the concert, and when we got home, he told me that he wants to start living his life not for himself but for God!" We rejoiced as much as you can over the phone, and when I got off the phone, I praised God for turning a Mother's Day that I had been dreading for her into one of indescribable praise! I loved my nephew's response when she told him that she was proud of him: "I didn't do a thing. God did it."!

After I'd finished penning this, I saw that I had a voice mail on my cell phone. The child whom we had been worried about had left a message on my phone, wishing me a happy Mother's Day.

Dear Lord, thank You for ministering to my brother and his family as only You can. Thank you for drawing my nephew to Yourself and for giving great hope to my sister-in-law, my brother, and myself on Mother's Day! As You know, my brother and sister-in-law can use the encouragement and hope right now. Please, Lord, continue to minister to them, and use others in their lives to reach out to them and love them.

CHAPTER 4

HOBBIES, RITUALS, AND ROUTINES

#BreakinThrough

It's better to have a partner than go it alone. Share
the work, share the wealth. And if one falls down
the other helps. But if there's no one to help, tough!

—Ecclesiastes 4:10 (NIV)

My husband and I bought our fourth and last—I promise you,
it's the last—"fixer-upper" house only a few years before the last of
our four children left home. In the middle of construction we had
three hurricanes pass right over our South Florida home. Yes, three!
Exhausted from all the damage in the aftermath, over a year later
we were finally getting to the last leg of our projects.

We had added on an office addition, and the last big project was
to sledgehammer our way through two concrete walls to open the
new addition to the existing house. My husband put on his mask to
cover his face and proceeded to pound his way through with a cut
saw and sledge hammer. I was busy in the kitchen preparing a crock
pot meal when he passed through, saying, "We are about to break
through," as if to let me know that he would like me to share this
moment with him. Realizing this, I put down *my* tools and came
with camera in hand.

As I arrived at his side, he explained to me that the beam under
the existing window was the dangerous part because of the weight

of it. I realized as he explained it to me that he was really happy that I had decided to share this moment with him. He has always been a high-energy guy and done a million projects, but I guess he thought this would be his last big project, and he wanted me to be a part of it. He had expressed that he most likely wouldn't take on any more major home renovations. Ironically, in an effort to get debt free, we took on one more after that—I hope the last fixer-upper!

Isn't it true that we all need cheerleaders to get us through this sometimes difficult life? Whether we are cooking a meal for our family or pounding through concrete walls, we all have that desire to share it with someone else. I believe listening is called an art because it doesn't come naturally to us. We'd rather talk about ourselves. I'm asking God to make me a better listener, and I am, thankfully, seeing some improvement. Not only is listening an art, I'm discovering, but it's a gift that is lasting.

Lord, thank You for Your design of marriage and family. I thank You that we don't have to go it alone, that we can be there to encourage and help each other do this life together.

#Chachis

> Do not store up for yourselves treasures on earth, where moth and rust destroy, and where thieves break in and steal, But store up for yourselves treasures in heaven, where moth and rust do not destroy, and where thieves do not break in and steal, For where you treasure is, there you heart will be also.
>
> —Matthew 6:19 (NIV)

I love to shop. I love color, and I love to look for accessories that I think will make our house a home. I look for things that have a special meaning to my husband and myself, things that may not mean anything to someone else. Those little somethings bring me a bit of happiness.

I know I'm not alone in enjoying this art of shopping. And I know that this isn't just a hobby strictly among the female species. There are even note cards and hand towels that joke about shopping and they are big sellers! They say things like, "I was going to clean house, but the stores were open" or "Does my insurance cover retail therapy?" There is a lot of pleasure in browsing, and I'm not talking computer talk! LOL.

Some of the things I have collected and purchased throughout the years have held up, but many have not, especially things that I have bought for the outside of my South Florida home. Knick-knacks, or *chachis*, as my friend calls them, make my backyard and patio areas look homey, but the warmth of the sun here is very hard on anything that lives outside. So I have really learned from experience what will survive outside and what won't. Not much will, but even though I've seen things wear out over and over again, there is still that allure, especially in the springtime, to create an enjoyable outside space for myself and my husband and any guests that might stop by. The marketing geniuses know that we won't stop buying: spring tablecloths, decorative lanterns, new patio umbrellas, citronella candles in decorative shapes, fun plastic wear in all kinds of fun, unimaginable summer colors, and fun pool toys.

Only about three years ago we bought some nice woven lawn chairs and then discovered the next spring that all the paint had worn off the arms and the weaving had all stretched out. They looked more than ten years old. I started digging where I keep my receipts, hoping to put my hands on the one I needed. I wanted to contact the manufacturers to see if they would stand behind their product, even though I assumed it was likely past a year's warranty. But I was aggravated. We had spent more than we usually do, because these had looked as if they would hold up, but they hadn't.

The same week that I was scrounging around for my receipt, I was reading a proverb for the day. It was Proverbs 111:10 (MSG). I stopped when I got to this part. "He manufactures truth and justice; All his products are guaranteed to last. Never out-of-date, never obsolete, rust-proof. All that he makes and does is honest and true: He paid the ransom for his people, He ordered his Covenant kept forever. He's so personal and holy, worthy of our respect. The good life begins in the fear of God—Do that and you'll know the blessing of God. His Hallelujah lasts forever!"

Thanks for the reminder that the only thing that will bring me fulfillment and joy and contentment that will last is You. I don't think You mind at all if we try to make our environment welcoming; You are the designer of all designers, but I do know that You, our Creator, not Your Creation, is what will bring us true and everlasting fulfillment.

#FragrantLife

But thank God! He has made us his captives and continues to lead us along in Christ's triumphal procession. Now he uses us to spread the knowledge of Christ everywhere, like a sweet perfume.

—2 Corinthians 2:14 (NLT)

My daily personal hygiene ritual includes washing my face with a skin cleanser. After learning that the product I had been using for years was supposedly not beneficial to the skin, I tried another one that a friend recommended.

This cleanser was touted as being one of the best for your skin. But I found it increasingly difficult to maintain my routine, because it was, well, boring, because it was fragrance free. I continued for weeks with this routine, but I found that I didn't look forward to it, and I found it difficult to continue my routine because of the lack of fragrance.

On a visit home, my twenty-year-old daughter, who is a cosmetologist and is in the know with all of these products, left her facial cleanser on the counter, so I helped myself.

Wow! It smelled magnificent, and the experience of cleansing my face suddenly became something that I looked forward to! I was amazed how just the smell of something could change my attitude toward a routine process.

Did you know that Christ was described as having an aroma and that "through His people spreads everywhere the fragrance of the knowledge of Himself"? (2 Corinthians 2:14–16). In Ephesians 5:2, the love that Christ has for us is described; we are challenged to be "a fragrant offering and sacrifice to God" for what He has done for us. That's why our lives are so meaningless and so filled with drudgery before we come to the place where we acknowledge our need for something greater than ourselves. It is then that we suddenly find a purpose-filled life.

But beware of the imitators of fragrance. I have a dresser top full of them, and they are costly. There are so many compelling distractions in our lives. They can be costly, as well. None of these imitators hold a stick to the non-fading, "real perfume" aroma of Christ Jesus, our Savior.

Thank You, Lord, for drawing me unto Yourself through the irresistible aroma of Your people!

#HeartofGod

So if you're serious about living this new resurrection life with Christ, act like it. Pursue the things over which Christ presides. Don't shuffle along, eyes to the ground, absorbed with the things right in front of you. Look up, and be alert to what is going on around Christ … that's where the action is. See things from his perspective.

—Colossians 3:1–2 (MSG)

A heaviness in my chest prompted me to go to my primary care doctor. With access to the Internet, and particularly Google, "knowledge" is at our fingertips, and my mind was allowing me to start imagining all of my symptoms and more!

At first I thought that it could be anxiety, but I have never really had an anxious-type personality. Then I started reading about the statin drug that I had been on and the "rare but possible" side effect of a lung disease. I also considered possible exposure to MRSA (infection by an antibiotic-resistant bacterium), as I had been doing some caregiving for a man who had tested positive for that. Now I was finding myself anxious!

After examining me, the doctor ruled out an infection, ordered a chest x-ray and suggested I try an antidepressant, to see if my symptoms would stop. I did and they didn't, so he suggested I go to a cardiologist to rule out any heart abnormalities.

That doctor, too, said he didn't hear anything abnormal and that my lungs were clear, but he would like to order a stress test just to make sure my heart was functioning normally, especially with the heart issues in my family history. So three appointments were made, for a rest test, a stress test, and a follow-up appointment.

I went for my routine walk the next morning with my headset on and was a little irritated at myself for finding myself irritated when I was stopped by a man in a moving van. He was looking for a particular house number. My normal response would have been to welcome an interruption as an opportunity to talk with someone, but not that day. I just wanted to listen to my favorite music and enjoy being alone. But wouldn't you know it, behind him was another woman whom I often met while walking, and I could tell that she wanted, of course, to talk to me this particular morning.

I removed my headset and walked over to her, saying to myself, "Not my will, Lord, but Yours." I just wanted to be alone one morning, but God had other plans. I have learned through the years not to ignore that small but powerful voice of the Holy Spirit.

The woman asked me how I was, and when I reciprocated by asking how she was doing, her tears started flowing. This is what she said to me. "I am eighty years old and I just found out that I'm codependent! I have a sister, and I've been trying to fix her. All I've been doing is crying, and I can't live my life this way. I am losing all of my friends!" I listened and agreed with her that we never quit learning. I told her encouragingly that it was wonderful she was participating in a program to help her overcome her codependency.

I recently found myself having a small pity party but pity party nonetheless. I had tried to share what I was going through with a woman who was going to have heart surgery. She was, understandably, so caught up with what she was having done that she hadn't even heard what I had said. The same week, I received an e-mail from a friend, asking me how I was really doing and how I could be prayed for. When I responded, I never heard back! Granted, maybe this person was so busy praying for me that they didn't have time to e-mail me, but I admit I'm skeptical. Told you I was feeling sorry for myself!

When I returned from my walk, I knew I needed some perspective, so I turned to scripture. I wasn't surprised when God spoke to me directly and personally through His written word. Psalm 26:1-3 says, "Clear my name, God; I've kept an honest shop. I've thrown in my lot with you, God, and I'm not budging. Examine me, God, from head to foot, order your battery of tests. Make sure I'm fit inside and out so I never lose sight of your love. But keep in step with you, never missing a beat." I realized that I had to remember the times when I've been so consumed with my own life and haven't been a good listener.

Yes, my exercise is important, to keep fit and to avoid some particular diseases that run in my family, but more important than my physical body is my spiritual condition. I really care more about it than the battery of tests the great physician orders for me. I want to be fit. *Fit* means never losing sight of how much He loves me and not missing any opportunities He has for me to share with others His great love. Yes, I listened today, reluctantly, to what He was calling me to do, and I had to stop my physical steps to keep in step with His plan, but I'm willing to bet that my heart didn't miss a beat during that ten minutes of rest!

Thank you, Lord, for your incredible love, even when we are selfish. I know it is good to be alone with you too, but when you make it quite clear by literally putting someone in my path, I thank You for Your spirit that dwells within and nudges me to do Your will and to die to mine.

#ListentoHisRhythm

Are you tired? Worn out? Burned out on religion? Come to me. Get away with me and you'll recover your life. I'll show you how to take a real rest. Walk with me and work with me … watch how I do it. Learn the unforced rhythms of grace. I won't lay anything heavy or ill-fitting on you. Keep company with me and you'll learn to live freely and lightly.

—Matthew 11:28–30 (MSG)

Happy New Year! I'm off, determined to start my new year with gusto and attempt to make some positive changes that we are all told are "musts."

As soon as I open my eyes, I start off by making my bed as soon as I step out of it. Done. Exercise is very important, so after brushing my teeth, I put on my clothes and head for my bicycle. Oh, I better put on my contacts so, in case my chain falls off, I will be able to see what I'm doing. I remember first to wash my hands, recalling that the doctor said that the solution is my best friend to avoid any eye infections. I ride for about twenty minutes; it's a good start. "They" say not to overdo if you're starting a new regime.

Coming back in my driveway with my bike, I see that the newspapers are piling up, so I decide to grab my cup of coffee and actually take the time to read the news. It feels wasteful if I buy the paper and don't read it—all those dead trees! My landscape-architect husband wouldn't approve. Feeling a bit guilty that it isn't decaf, I grab a cup of coffee, with no-fat cream and, okay, I admit it, sweeten it with real sugar. I sit in my recliner, something I never thought I'd get to do. I take a break and browse through the paper, where I read about the value of a pedometer to track your steps. Ten thousand steps should be one's goal—and that's if one doesn't have weight to lose!

Okay, now it's time for my morning hygiene routine. I cleanse my face, tone it, and moisturize it, of course, and head for the shower. Then I have to make a decision whether to use the clay shampoo or the gray highlighter shampoo or the dandruff shampoo. (Come to think of it, my kids have been brushing my shoulders when I wear black.) Then to the bottle of mousse my daughter got me, and the root toner. And on to drying, reminding myself of the words of my daughter, the cosmetologist. "Mom, you have to be patient. Your hair won't look good if you shortcut this process." Done. Those bangs are getting a bit long, and my daughter does say that to keep a good style you need to get a good cut at least every five to six weeks. I need to schedule that.

Now to pick out some clothes and the right shoes. We are told that pointed shoes elongate short bodies, and that is what I have. What do I do with all of my other, non-pointed, shoes, which I was perfectly content with until I heard that?

Oh, dear, I haven't eaten and it is important to eat right and to get that metabolism off and running. I'm so proud of myself that I go for my oat granola, topped with strawberries and bananas, and a glass of orange juice. Okay, I admit that I forgot the bran that my mother has been encouraging me to take for regularity. I'll take an extra scoop tomorrow. As I write this, I remember that I forgot to take my Vitamin C, my multivitamin, and my fish oil. I'm working on that cholesterol, to avoid meds. Okay, on to my day. Now it is 10:30 a.m. Let's see, due bills were paid yesterday, I have chicken left over to put on a salad for dinner tonight, I have a few more Christmas thank-you notes to write, some e-mails to respond to, and if I can get to organizing tax information, that would be good. My husband keeps telling me to drop everything and work on the book that I want to write, but I need to get my vehicle taken in for that recall issue, and what about all those back-in-the-day photos that I want to put in my "creative memory" books—and I still need to learn how to file all those digital photos!

I should be planning that brunch I want to have to encourage new women in our area, and I have some friends whom I want to catch up with. Organization! My, there is certainly a need for that around here. I must sign up for that adult ed class on getting organized. It seems the harder I try the behinder I get!

I still have my makeup to put on, very important at my age, and I haven't done my Bible reading for the day. Hmm, maybe that will help me figure out what is most important for me to accomplish today. I'll be back and let you know if I found any answers.

I read of Abraham and his desire to find among his people a wife for his son. I learn how God answered his prayers and gave him the desire of his heart. I have two unmarried sons and a daughter. I stop to pray for their future wives and husband and for my future daughters-in-law and son-in-law. In Proverbs 9:11, I read, "For through me your days will be many, and years will be added to your life."

Yes, I'll do what I can to take care of my body. Believe me, it won't be done perfectly, but I am reminded that even the length of my life is ultimately purposefully determined for me. Despite what you hear, all the oatmeal in the world can't extend my life or yours beyond the day the Savior calls us to our real home, where the one thing we can count on is life being simplified!

Lord, thank You for the reminder that making time with You as my first priority will silence all the other things tugging at me and give me the ability to silence all the other voices. Then I will be able to clearly hear Your voice and *only* Your voice, because that is what I really want to do today—exactly what you are calling me to.

#Maintenance

He manufactures truth and justice; all his products are guaranteed to last … Never out-of-date, obsolete, rust-proof. All that he makes and does is honest and true: He paid the ransom for his people.

—Psalm 111:7–9 (MSG)

As I type this, I am sitting and waiting, along with lots of other people, for my car to be maintained. Maintenance is something that can't be avoided in a world where things just wear out, especially this consumer world, where things are now *designed* to last for a shorter period of time.

It has been one of those weeks during which maintenance seems to be the theme. Thankfully, we made it through Thanksgiving dinner with our family and no appliance failures. We have experienced power failures before with the big bird in the oven. A few days after Thanksgiving my husband asked me whether I had spilled something in the garage or the dishwasher was leaking. So, after a full day of working, he decided to start the process of dismantling the machine to see if he could discover why it was malfunctioning.

He gathered his tools and a flashlight, which I held for him as he meticulously unscrewed the eight or so screws around the top of the housing, which contained more rubber gaskets and more plastic parts. He strategically placed the screws and parts so he would remember the order in which he had disassembled them. We got to the bottom of the pump, where he thought something might have lodged that was preventing it from draining. Sure enough, there were some pieces of glass, so he removed them and started to reinstall the final pump cover. Finally everything was in its proper place, with no extra screws. He gave it a test run, and it drained!

We high-fived each other over the successful process. We had one last "simple" test, realigning the washer so that the final screws at the front of the machine would align with the existing holes to secure it in place. The hardest part was over—or so we thought. It was difficult to see, so as I was shining the flashlight while he was trying to get the screw in the hole, I offered to help—and the screw slipped off the tool and fell into the dishwasher, partially into one of the holes surrounding the plastic disc that we had just disassembled and reassembled! Simultaneously we cried, "No-o-o!" Of course, the phone started ringing at the same time, just to add a bit more anxiety to the situation. We ignored the phone, and my husband pleaded, "Don't touch anything! I'll be back." He came back with a handy little tool that had a hook on the end, but no luck. He left again with the same admonition: "Don't touch anything!" and this time came back with another hooked tool. We held our breaths while he tried it. The little hook grabbed the screw and removed it quite handily!

I was reminded of the scripture from my ladies' Bible study that morning. I don't know if that scripture had this kind of thing in mind, but I was going to apply it to all that this week had for us. "I have told you these things so that in me you may have peace. In this world you will have trouble. But take heart! I have overcome the world" (John 16:33 NIV). Our circumstances can be very frustrating at times. We can't avoid trouble, but we can decide how we will react to it. I watched in amazement as my husband just took one step at a time in his problem solving and saw how his perseverance paid off. He could have gotten frustrated, but he didn't.

I thought of a man I'd met at a local soup kitchen who, in spite of difficult circumstances, was always so pleasant. I had actually just had a conversation with him about his demeanor and had shared with him that I appreciated his cheerfulness. Another woman, who sat next to me at the auto dealer's, started talking to me about her background. She told me how her husband had died at a very young age from a wartime-inflicted disease and how she had raised two young children by herself, working two jobs to provide for them. She was now retired and living in a condo on the beach, which her children had bought for a vacation home and had allowed her to live in for the past twenty years. I empathized with how difficult that must have been for her, and she said, "It was hard at the time, but I am so lucky—" She caught herself in midsentence and explained that her mother had always told her that there was no such thing as luck. Then she continued, "God really walked with me through that time. I don't know where I'd be without my children."

Lord, thank You for a husband who walks with You and, because of that walk, faces all the uncertainties in this world one step at a time, trusting that You will help him—yes, even with the home-maintenance issues. Thanks for being a personal God who cares about even these little details and helps us get through them in peace!

#PerfectlyKnittedinLove

For you created my inmost being; you knit me together in my mother's womb. I praise you because I am fearfully and wonderfully made; your works are wonderful, I know that full well. My frame was not hidden from you when I was made in the secret place. When I was woven together in the depths of the earth, your eyes saw my unformed body. All

the days ordained for me were written in your book
before one of them came to be.

—Psalm 139:13–16 (NIV)

I never thought of myself as a perfectionist, until I recently
learned the new skill of knitting from my mom. I was all excited that
I was actually going to attempt my first real garment, a baby's hat.

I decided a visit from my mom was a good time to tackle the
project, as she would be able to help me with the questions I knew
would come. It seemed a good idea because I was making lots of
errors and was clueless on how to fix them. My mom knew how to
correct my mistakes, but even after watching her, I was unprepared
to get out of the tangled predicaments I found myself in. My mom
assured me that all knitters made mistakes and that if they told me
otherwise they were not being truthful.

Well, Mom went home, and after hours of ripping out, and
starting over, and lack of sleep, and sore fingertips, I decided to take
it slow and try one last time to complete this project perfectly. I got
well past the halfway point with the correct number of stitches,
and I was feeling quite smug and encouraged that maybe it was
indeed possible to get through this error free! Well, the dreaded
mistake came, and I was too far along to rip it out, so I decided to
try to pick up some dropped stitches. To my surprise, and thanks
to the forgiveness of the yarn I was using, the flaw really wasn't that
noticeable.

As I was knitting, I was thinking a lot about the mom-to-be
whom I was knitting the hat for. As I knitted I prayed for her and the
daughter she was expecting; I prayed that He would walk with her
through this time. You see, this young mom-to-be hadn't planned
the pregnancy, and for the time being it looked as though she was
going to be a single mom.

Psalm 29 took on new meaning for me as I was working and
thinking about this precious child being knitted in her mother's

womb. I don't know who discovered knitting or who came up with the unique patterns, but knowing the detail and intricacy required for knitting gave me a new appreciation for accomplished knitters— and, for that matter, anyone who knit at all! But even more, it pointed me to the giver of human life Himself and provided a greater understanding of the depth of love he has for his children; he hand sculpted each of us from nothing into a person! How appropriate that the word *knit* is used in scripture to describe the complexity of human life! As a new knitter, trust me when I say it's complicated, but it's nothing compared to the way we were created!

Lord, thank You for the incredible way that You chose to bring new life into your world. Thank you for telling us "He knows us far better than we know ourselves, knows our pregnant condition and keeps us present before God. That's why we can be so sure that every detail in our lives of love for God is worked into something good" (Romans 8:27–28 MSG). Be with this mom-to-be, and give her extra strength as she welcomes this new magnificent creation of Yours into this world. I am thankful that our flaws don't come as a surprise to You but that You take them and work them for our good.

#PickleballBuds

> He answered, "Love the Lord your God with all your heart and with all your soul and with all your strength and with all your mind" and "Love your neighbor as yourself."

> —Luke 10:27 (NIV)

I had heard about pickleball several years ago at my parent's retirement community. I had also had heard the unique *pong* sound in the distance as people played, kind of like that popping sound you make when you put your index finger inside your cheek and then pop it out!

After a recent surgery, I was ready to attempt playing tennis again. I was all excited when I saw some women gathering at our community's tennis courts, so I strolled over to see if they would be interested in another player. They explained to me that they were playing this game called pickleball. They were fairly new at the game themselves, and they welcomed me to join them. Their enthusiasm for the game and their welcoming spirit was such an encouragement to me after I'd been diagnosed with cancer and undergone the removal of one of my kidneys. Though I tried to explain it to them, they really had no way of knowing what a pivotal part they played in restoring me emotionally.

The first thing I noticed was that the scoring was quite different and much more complicated than in tennis, but they were patient and kept assuring me that I would soon learn the rules and scoring.

I was learning, and I was digging the verbiage. How could I not enjoy a game whose number-1 rule requires you to stay out of the kitchen; number 2 says that when you have the ball you are queen; and number 3, specifies that you have to do a hit and run when returning to the queen's court. Count me in!

It was fun to get back to some physical exercise and at the same time meet some new neighbors. It just so happened that they were all moms of adult children, who were just out for some fun while exercising and sharing each other's burdens, as well.

During a water break, one of the youngest moms was telling us of her frustration that her son, who was looking for a job but hadn't heard from a place where he had submitted a job resume. She looked at three of the "older" moms and asked if we thought she should call the employer herself. We broke into laughter when all three of us responded simultaneously with "No-o-o!" I took it that all three of us were seasoned moms, and it was good to be with these women, to sort out parenting and grandparenting responsibilities.

Thank you, Lord, for allowing me to meet these new women at a time when I needed some exercise as well as camaraderie.

#RoutineDoldrums

> Make every effort to live in peace with all men and to be holy; without holiness no one will see the Lord. See to it that no one misses the grace of God and that no bitter root grows up to cause trouble and defile many.

> —Hebrews 12:14–15 (NIV)

My daughter, who had been married a few short months, called one morning to chat and to share what had been going on in her life—or, more accurately, what had not been going on.

She expressed that she had been down, but couldn't put her finger on why. She explained that she and her husband had talked and had come up with a plan in hopes of changing her mood. I knew then I liked this new son-in-law! He was a man with a plan to resolve things before they turned into a crisis. I couldn't help, to the chagrin of my daughter, but feel a little sorry for my son-in-law. It was okay for me to be cranky with my husband and have him discouraged by my unhappiness, but I hated to see this young man have to go through it!

She said that they had decided to schedule a date night once a week and a one-night getaway on a monthly basis, which they would plan in turns. She said that they'd agreed to continue their search for a church and desired to become part of a group where they could get together with other couples in the same stage of life to share life's journey with. And because of their busy work schedules, he suggested professional help with cleaning their home, to take some of the pressure off!

It was exciting to see them working through their issues of learning to live with someone new. I found myself reminiscing about when my husband and I first started our lives together, the ups and downs and the way we worked through some of very same issues.

When the wedding is over and the hard work begins, the routineness of our lives can tend to get us down, because life is, well, just repetitious. I remember complaining about my frustration with cleaning the house and then the next day repeating the same steps. My husband would wisely explain that so many of our days are just routine. "That it is just part of life; everything becomes undone, and we just do it again tomorrow." I think he probably added some comment about our messy house being an argument against evolution resulting in progress. The only evolution is a devolution, just as our home doesn't keep getting tidied up and evolve into something better. It is deteriorating and being destroyed by rust and mold as I speak!

I am giving thanks today for a son-in-law who saw the wisdom in trying to add some diversions from routine to their lives, to make things more interesting. And I'm proud of a daughter who chose honesty rather than sulking, who voiced her concerns so that resentment wouldn't have a chance to take root.

Lord, thank You for Your design of marriage and family. Thank You for our daughter and son-in-law's relationship and desire to walk together as a team. Thank You for the way that we grow in You as we learn to die to ourselves and serve our spouses. Thanks for loving us through the times that we are growing and for the amazing benefits of perseverance.

#ScallopHunters

Then God said, "Let the waters swarm with fish and other life. Let the skies be filled with birds of every kind." So God created great sea creatures

and every living thing that scurries and swarms in
the water, and every sort of bird—each producing
offspring of the same kind. And God saw that it was
good. Then God blessed them, saying, "Be fruitful
and multiply. Let the fish fill the seas, and let the
birds multiply on the earth." And evening passed
and morning came, marking the fifth day.

—Genesis 1:20–23 (NLT)

One of our all-time favorite vacations, when our children were
old enough to swim, was to go bay scalloping. This involves getting
into the gulf with a mask and snorkel and looking for mollusks,
which hide in the tall grasses and sandy bottoms.

We are thrilled that our kids enjoyed it so much, and we are now
scalloping with our adult kids and our grandchildren.

In God's amazing design, the scallop shell has hundreds of
iridescent blue eyeballs around the outline of the shell, which can
be easily seen if the sunbeams are streaming at just the right angle
in the water.

I have tried to decide why it is so much fun. For one thing, you
are under the water, looking at the variety of creatures—starfish, sea
horses, bait fish, blowfish, crabs—and myriads of types of vegetation
and coral. And it is quiet. The only sound you hear is your own
breathing through the snorkel. It is lot like an Easter egg hunt. You
know the shape of the scallop, so you glide through the water while
your eyes are looking back and forth until you recognize the unique
shape, and then you dive down to scoop him up!

It is a great vacation for families with lots of children, as they
can all be in the water working toward a common purpose. You
hunt, you gather, you clean, and you eat them together. Our most
recent trip included two of our kids and their spouses and our five
grandchildren, all in the water. All but the two littlest ones were
gathering—that is, until two of our grandsons started swimming

under the boat and filling up the nets of the youngest two as they dangled them in the water, so they would feel like they were participating. They were thrilled to be catching, and their parents were getting a break too. It was so much fun with so many of us, and we all enjoyed being together. Our youngest granddaughter, who is four, even participated in the cleaning of the scallops.

God didn't intend for us to do life alone. I think scalloping is one of the greatest examples of living in community. You have a common purpose, you help one another, you have more eyes to watch for dangerous situations, and there is much laughter. Together you help each other maneuver through the scallop field while being anchored together, and at the end of the day your gather to break bread as you share the catch of the day, the tasty scallop morsels.

Lord, thank You for the design of the family and for creating us to need one another. Thank You too for Your church and for the community of believers who work together for the common purpose of glorifying You and protecting each other while doing life together.

#SoundofSilence

For the Lord your God is living among you. He is a mighty savior. He will take delight in you with gladness. With his love, he will calm all your fears. He will rejoice over you with joyful songs.

—Zephaniah 3:17 (NLT)

I decided to get up this morning and mix up my morning exercise routine. If I don't, I tend to get bored. I'm not by nature an individual of routine.

I decided to take a bicycle ride instead of a walk and to do the "country" block, which requires going along a pretty major highway. When I do the full block, I usually do the highway part on the tail end, but I decided to get it over first this time, so I wouldn't be dreading it and could enjoy the rest of the ride.

I had my headphones on and started pedaling. I was bummed because the highway noise was so loud that I couldn't make out the words, even with the volume at its peak. It was so loud that I even took my phone out a couple of times to make sure it wasn't dead. As I rode, I pushed my earpieces deeper into my ears in an effort to make out some of the words and drown out the roar of traffic. It was deafening, and I found myself full of, well, maybe not anxiety but certainly unrest.

I finally made it to the corner where I turned, and with the simple left-hand turn, everything changed. Things greened up, trees flanked both sides of the road, and the quiet was instantaneous. I could feel my body relaxing, and the sound of my praise music was coming in loud and clean. *Ahhh, this is so much better.*

I remember struggling with having more alone time after my last child left to begin his adult life. I didn't think I would ever get used to the quiet. Let me tell you that I was wrong! In fact, I have grown to crave my quiet time as I never thought possible.

Let me encourage you to daily find a place away from the "road noise." This world is such a busy place, and with all the technology, it won't be slowing down anytime soon.

In my effort to hear the music, I was reminded in quite a practical way of how difficult it is to hear the Spirit of God when there is so much noise around us. I don't want to miss what God has to say to me through his word, and the only way to prevent that from happening is to start out my day by getting alone with Him and asking Him to speak to me and direct my day through the manual he has left us. There are so many other things and people clamoring for our time and attention.

Lord, thank You for the practical ways You teach me. Your word tells me that You even know the numbers of hairs on my head. You often reveal yourself to me through practical examples that I can understand. I shouldn't be surprised that You even know the way I learn best, my particular learning style. Thank You for the reminder that all the noise prevents me from hearing what You have to share with me. Thank You for helping me to not only adjust to the quietness of this stage of life but to relish my times with You.

#Teatime

How sweet are your words to my taste, sweeter than honey to my mouth!

—Psalm 119:103 (NIV)

Throughout the years I have been more of a coffee drinker than a tea drinker, but in my later years I have decided that teatime is something I would like to fit into my daily routine.

I say routine, because like anything else, if we aren't intentional about something we want to add to our lives, it most likely won't happen.

I even have a collection of teacups that were my grandmother's, so now that the children are grown, I think I will start a special time in the afternoon to savor a cup of hot tea! I think I'll have my first official teatime with her violet teacup, which I remember seeing in her dish cupboard. I wonder if my grandmother started her teatime when her children left home and she was a new grandmother. Maybe it's a stage-of-life thing.

An older woman whom I care for reminded me of this desire. She had a ceramic goose teapot that she had used throughout the years for her teatime. She and her husband had hot green tea every evening with their dinner. It happened because it was part of their scheduled day. How did I know it was a routine? I could see the years of tea stains on the goose's mouth, the spout. And I knew it had become a special time for her and her husband, because when I went to heat the water in the individual cups in the microwave, she suggested that I use the goose. It was familiar, it was a habit, it was comforting, and so I heated the water, filled up the goose, and served their tea.

I desire to know more of God's word in the same way. I want it to be so familiar, so habit forming, and so comforting that my Bible, like the ceramic goose teapot, will be covered with my fingerprints and have, maybe not tea stains, but tear stains dripped on the pages, from when I have carried everything to my "Father [who] Knows Best!"

Dear Lord, thank You for not leaving us here without instructions. Thank You for Your word that guides and comforts us and gives us hope for the future.

#UniqueDifferences

Because of the privilege and authority God has given me, I give each of you this warning: Don't think you are better than you really are. Be honest in your evaluation of yourselves, measuring yourselves by the faith God has given us. Just as our bodies have many parts and each part has a special function, so it is with Christ's body. We are many parts of one body, and we all belong to each other. In his grace, God has given us different gifts for doing certain things well.

—Romans 12:3–6 (NLT)

Are you one of those people who freak out when your routine is disrupted? I'm not one of those people. Gotcha! I have to make a concentrated effort to stay on task, so breaks in my routine are, well, just part of my routine. I'm sure if I had a label it would say "attention deficit disorder," although I have never been diagnosed. I have learned to compensate for my "disorder." Now, if I could just get others living around me to accept me!

I get bored and overwhelmed with cleaning the house, so I have found a way to make it fun. When I make the decision to begin, I start wherever I am—kind of like ready, set, go!—and start putting things away. This may lead me to one of our three bedrooms, or a bathroom, or a closet, or the garage, or outside in the gazebo, or talking to a friend on the phone, or out to the mall. I don't get bored because I am walking all over the house and even getting some fresh air once in a while. They say walking and fresh air are both good for you.

I even passed on my cleaning skills to my four children. When everyone left the table, I would tell them to put so many things away, based on their various ages. Hey, it was a game, and the task didn't seem so overwhelming. Of course, when they were teens, eighteen things seemed like a lot to them. At least they knew where the beginning and ending of their duties were. I can hear them telling their spouses, "That's it, honey. I've put twenty-six things away, and I'm finished." Sorry, daughter-in-law!

I do become a bit frazzled, though, when I can't do habitual things, like flush the toilet because of a saturated drain field. I also can't wash clothes when this happens, and I can't run the dishwasher or even take a leisurely bath, anything that involves flushing water down the system. There is always the refrigerator to be cleaned out, but why would I? Everything is fitting! I could go through piles of papers, but I know where to locate things in those piles.

So, I'm actually kind of glad when this occurs, because I am absolved from false guilt about not doing what that little voice in my head tells me I *should* do. Instead, I can feel free to do something fun, like writing about my feelings. A lot of women like *talking* about their feelings, and I like that too, but when I *write* about them, I have a captive audience—they listen. Speaking of captive audiences, it must be my stage of mothering, because right now I feel as if none of my kids really want to listen to what I have to say. That's why I decided to volunteer at a local boot camp for boys who have gotten into trouble with the law. They are hoping for help to change their lifestyles and be placed back into the community with new purpose. I only go once a week, and I can't believe it, but the young man I see is actually happy to see me! Of course my eighteen-year-old says, "It's because he's in jail, Mom. He doesn't have a choice!"

After that I have to repeat to myself, "I am fearfully and wonderfully made!"

Routines are frankly for people who don't know how to have a fun or are here on this earth to drive the rest of us crazy! I'm sorry. You are fearfully and wonderfully made as well, and now we both just have to learn how to get along!

Lord, thank You for making me just the way You did. Help me to know that it's okay to be me and that cleaning my house is low on the list of things that really matter in life. Help me to be understanding of others who are very different from me, and help me to accept them just the way they are.

CHAPTER 5

HELP WITH BURDENS

#BlindCurve

Don't brag about tomorrow, since you don't know
what the day will bring.

—Proverbs 27:1 (NLT)

I had to force myself to walk one morning, as I just didn't feel
like getting out there and doing it. But knowing it was good for me
and good for my heart, I made myself do it.

This one winding road that I walk down is tucked beneath a
tropical canopy of shade trees and palms. As I was making my way
around one curve, I saw a sign that read Blind Curve. It is such a
sharp curve that you would have no idea until a car was right on you
that there could be a vehicle coming your way. I hugged the edge of
the road as I rounded the curve.

I couldn't help but think of our lives and the blind curves that
we face each day. None of us know what a day will bring or what is
around the corner in our lives.

The next day I had a better understanding of why I hadn't felt
up to a walk. I had a miserable night of tossing and turning, with
fever followed by chills as my body tried to fight off an infection.
Every muscle ached, and my head pounded, and my chest felt as if
it had a brick on top of it. I knew that I would spend the next few
days, even possibly a week, trying to regain strength.

My husband, who had gone through this the prior week, acknowledged that I had gotten it worse than he had. I was relieved to hear him say that, as I had been feeling wimpy, knowing that he had managed to go in to work. A friend was cajoling me to be strong for the "cause" of women (you know how women say that men are babies when they are sick). I told her that I was sorry but I had failed miserably. I had gladly accepted and would continue to accept all the help that came my way. This wasn't the time to prove a point about my valor as a woman.

I thought of one of the women in my Bible study group who had just completed chemo treatments, and I wondered how her body had felt during those treatments and how she had endured it. I thought of two other friends and my son-in-law, who lived with the daily pain associated with the debilitating diseases of rheumatoid and psoriatic arthritis. I thought of the elderly woman I had met at the grocery, who was in her late eighties; she managed to plug along daily with very little complaining as her body deteriorated. I thought of my dad and how toward the end of his life even the simplest act of breathing had become so painful for him and how exhausted he had been. There were so many people living with pain. Then I thought of the pain that my Savior had suffered. What I was experiencing, and which was making me so miserable, couldn't even be compared to what He had willingly suffered on our behalf. Fully God, fully man, he took on the pain that we deserved out of his great love for us. At one point he asked for the "cup" to be removed. "Father, if you are willing, take this cup from me; yet not my will, but yours be done" (Luke 22: 42 NIV).

After a fall on the tennis court which led to an ultrasound, a cancerous tumor on my kidney was discovered. This was another blind curve in my life. My father had it as well, at approximately the age that I am now. One day I was living my life, and in the following weeks I was scheduling surgery to remove a kidney. At this writing, I am thankful that it isn't in any other organ. Time will tell whether it will ever show up elsewhere.

Dear Lord, I thank You that we don't know what lies ahead in our lives. I am thankful that, just as You entrusted Your life to Your Father, we can entrust our lives to you. Help me to live out each day doing Your will for that day and not to worry about the future.

#Disconnected

Who of you by worrying can add a single hour to his life?

—Matthew 6:27 (NIV)

My husband owns his own small business and, with a sluggish economy, is forced to be a "Johnny do it all." He is responsible for all aspects of the business, from the work itself to the appointment making to the billing. Because of the wide range of responsibilities, it is a lot to keep track of.

One particular morning was not that different from other mornings—except that he had forgotten to take his cell phone. I knew that the consequences would be greater than usual, as he was headed south to Miami for the day. That meant he would be without communication for the entire day.

Right away I thought of myself and how this would affect my day. (I know—it's all about me!) I knew that the only way he would be able to connect with me would be by borrowing a phone. There are no more phone booths along the way, the way we used to stay in touch. I was a little agitated that I would be inconvenienced on that day, but then I quickly decided to pray for him, as I was sure he was being hard enough on himself over adding this kink to his day.

That was confirmed when I saw a Miami area code on his phone and answered the call for him. The person whom he was to meet with at 7:30 a.m. was running thirty minutes behind. He would be forced to wait, unknowing.

The second call came in from an employee who was working in another location and had a question about a drawing. He said that he would make a decision on the question he had, and if it wasn't right, it could be changed later.

Hmm, maybe being without constant attachment to a mobile phone would actually make for a peace-filled day for him. I decided to pray along those lines. "Lord, take his anxiousness away and guide his steps throughout the day. Give him your peace and protection while he is on the road. Please bring him safely home to me tonight."

It would be a long day for me, as the unknown of his whereabouts and his safety would leave me a bit anxious. But I had experienced that for years, and I just trusted in God's protection of him. "Lord, please give me that peace that is beyond human understanding. Help me to trust that he is in Your care and that You will bring him home safely."

Maybe cells phones have given us the illusion of a sense of power, the feeling that we can control our lives.

Dear Lord, thanks for the reminder that You are the giver of life and help me to rest today and every day, trusting in your sovereignty and knowing that, whether my husband comes home tonight or not, you will still be the anchor of my soul. "Jesus Christ: the same yesterday, and today, and forever" (Hebrews 13–8).

#GodsCall

And we know that in all things God works for the good of those who love him, who have been called according to his purpose.

—Romans 8:28 (NIV)

Our eldest child was six, our daughter four, and our baby eleven months when my husband and I learned in a most difficult way what "releasing a child" meant.

Oh, we had been taught that our children were gifts, loaned to us by God. I understood this intellectually; I even spoke often of this truth. But I'm one of those persons who has to experience something firsthand to really understand the concept. I believe today's educators would label me a tactile learner.

It was in May of 1985 when our eleven-month-old son, who had been walking a mere week, opened the back door of our home, toddled into the family swimming pool, and nearly drowned. My mother, who was visiting for Mother's Day, found him. He was completely unconscious, bloated with water, and blue from the lack of oxygen.

In response to my 911 call, an Oakland Park, Florida, police officer, Robert Touhey, who was providentially passing our street during his lunch hour, was the first to respond to the call. He did get a pulse on our baby after administering CPR, and then an ambulance rushed him to the hospital. They were considering a tracheotomy, but upon our pediatrician arriving and observing him, he advised them to wait.

Our son remained in a coma state that evening, and we prayed that God would allow us to have him back. My prayer was to let him live, no matter what his condition; his daddy's prayer to God was to bring him back whole or to take him home. Our child did awake twenty-four hours later, and brain scans confirmed that he was indeed, whole.

Until you've been so close to losing a child or until you've lost a child—which I am unable to imagine the pain of—you can't explain how you are suddenly forced to turn that child over to God. If you have lost a child, I know you have a deeper understanding of God's grace than I do.

That was my entire hope and strength in that moment, knowing that the God of the universe was in complete control. He had created this child, loved this child, and was in control of what was going to happen to this child, physically as well as spiritually. I can't imagine going through anything like this without this security and hope.

We also struggled through a compound fracture of our son's arm when he was four. A fall off a slide in a park resulted in a break requiring two surgeries, two different hospital stays, and a year of therapy. We were told by doctors that they were going to study his arm, as they had never seen that bad a break on that young a child. We would have to have annual x-rays taken to see how or if his arm would grow properly.

The Lord just kept forcing us to be reminded that this child—and all of our children—were in bigger hands than ours.

I have notes written in Acts from a sermon I once heard about turning points in our lives. These were the main parts: "Turning points occur during normal occurrences of our lives. These turning points are usually sudden, unexpected; some are positive and some negative, but they always leave us surprised. Our family and others are impacted, and it prompts changes in us that are surprising to others."

That was me after nearly losing our son. All the theology in the world couldn't speak to me as that experience had. What did I learn? I learned that my son was not mine but God's. I learned that we had absolutely no control over whether our child was going to live or die. God was holding that child's life in His hands, just as He does daily with all children. But you can't understand this until you see how quickly that God-given life can be taken away. We want to think we are in control, but we aren't. It is during these times that everything is put into perspective and God's sovereignty is clear. It is a reminder: "Hey, remember I'm here, and I have everything under control. Trust me."

Dear Lord, we are so grateful that You heard our cries to heal our son and that You gave him back to us. I know that things could have turned out much differently. We have witnessed and read of many similar situations that didn't turn out with a happy ending. I have often wondered how we would have reacted had he not survived. I believe that You would have walked with us through whatever we had to face. Whether a situation turns out as we think best or not, You remain trustworthy.

Our family was invited to Officer Touhey's surprise retirement party in 1995, where our son and he were reunited for the first time since the accident. Officer Touhey served for twenty-five years on the Oakland Park police department. Our son is now thirty-two years old and makes a living on the water. His middle name is

Robert; he's named after my dad, but we found it ironic that it was also the name of the police officer who revived him! Our family will be forever grateful to Officer Bob Touhey and his family.

#HopeforTomorrow

Why am I discouraged? Why is my heart so sad? I will put my hope in God! I will praise him again— my Savior and my God!

—Psalm 42:11 (NLT)

Have your circumstances ever left you feeling hopeless? If you are a parent or grandparent, have you ever looked at the lives of your children or grandchildren and decisions they were making and felt despair?

I have been there, but I have climbed out of that joyless spot by calling out to the one who defines *hope*.

I was reminded of this great hope the other day, as I was weeding in my South Florida landscape in the middle of the summer. My hands were deep in the dirt, gripping the roots of some aggressive weeds, when I stumbled across an old rock that I had placed under the tree months before. It had worked its way into the dirt, and as I brushed away the soil from the crevices of the engraved letters, the word *hope* emerged.

I had been through a particular difficult week, and I was having trouble climbing out of a feeling of hopelessness. I turned to my Bible for some strength and encouragement. It was the twenty-eighth of the month, so I started in the gospel of Matthew and went to the last chapter, which was the twenty-eighth. It was entitled The Resurrection. It describes how Mary Magdalene and the "other" Mary went to look at the tomb. They couldn't have been more down than at this point. They had watched their Savior be tortured and crucified and were grieving that He was seemingly gone forever. They went to the tomb where, to their great surprise, an angel met them and said, "Do not be afraid, for I know that you are looking for Jesus, who was crucified. He is not here; he has risen, just as he said. Come and see the place where he lay. Then go quickly and tell his disciples. He has risen from the dead and is going ahead of you into Galilee."

Then I was reminded: the resurrection of Jesus is our hope. There is no other hope. Hope emerged from a grave. If He was a mere man, he would have been just another dead man. But He was who He claimed to be all along. He was God in the flesh, who had come to this earth as a child and walked here for thirty years to teach and heal. But His most important calling, his purpose, was the sacrifice that we needed for the forgiveness of sins. We would have no forgiveness of sins if he hadn't given His life. But he didn't stay dead. He was resurrected, and all we have to do is trust that He is who He said He was, and we will one day join Him for eternity.

When days seem dark and circumstances feel desperate, confess your lack of trust in God to work in your life and the lives of your children and grandchildren. Ask Him to give you the ability to go by your feelings less and less and trust in Him more and more. He did it for me; He'll do it for you!

Lord, forgive me when my hope tank is on empty and I continue on with my own strength, not stopping to fill up on your word, running the risk of complete hopelessness. Thank you for the tangible reminder that You are the embodiment of hope.

#LearningtoWalk

Come to me, all who are weary and burdened, and I will give you rest. Take my yoke upon you and learn from me, for I am gentle and humble in heart, and you will find rest for your souls. For my yoke is easy and my burden is light.

—Matthew 11:28-30 (NIV)

An empty nester for a few short years, I believe that I have experienced the gamut of experiences that come with being a mom. (Per Dictionary.com, gamut means "The entire scale or ranges: the gamut of dramatic emotions from grief to joy.")

One of my sons gave me a badge to wear at my fiftieth birthday party that read "I've survived nearly everything." My husband and I have had the conversation that the only thing we haven't experienced is the death of a child. We came close to losing a child and walked through the unknown of whether this child would live or die, and that was bad enough. Knowing how difficult that was, and knowing that with the great number of children our odds of experiencing this increase, we have discussed how we would live through that. This may seem like an odd conversation, but because I'm a mom and know in my mind that this would be the most difficult thing to live through, I like to talk about it rather than pretend that the possibility doesn't exist.

My brother and sister-in-law, who have five boys, are just a few years behind us in the process of raising their children. We have shared our parenting experiences with each other throughout the years.

This year, my brother and his wife began blazing a trail that we have not walked down, and we are learning from them. Just a short twenty-five days ago, they had to live through the ordeal of looking for their missing fourth son, Preston. Then they learned that he had taken his own life, a couple weeks short of his fourteenth birthday.

How do you go on with life as you know it after experiencing such a heart-wrenching tragedy? Throughout the initial days of grieving and walking through what had to be done, my sister-in-law said it all when she said over and over, "I couldn't do this without my Savior."

Skeptics are quick to spout off that Christianity is just a crutch. And I would respond, what is a crutch? Dictionary.com says, "A prop for the lame." Lame means "Powerless, impotent, without satisfactory or decisive effect." When you have lost a child, you are powerless to change the outcome. As a parent, you would do everything within your power to change the result. As my brother kept saying, "I wish I had a second chance to help him get through whatever he was going through."

My nephew's pastor put it so well at his memorial service, explaining that he had made a really poor decision the day he followed through with taking his life and that in his youth, he was not capable of realizing all the pain that he would bring to family and friends. But the pastor then shared that our nephew had made an earlier decision to receive the forgiveness offered through the shedding of the blood of Jesus Christ. We have a merciful and forgiving and trustworthy God, and His word tells us, "For by grace you have been saved through faith. And this is not our own doing; it is the gift of God, not a result of works, that that no one may boast" (Ephesians 2:8–9 ESV). We either get to heaven by following all the Old Testament laws perfectly, which is humanly impossible, or we recognize and accept the sacrifice that was made for us. This is the *gospel*—the good news—explained simply enough for a child to understand. Jesus paid it all. Recognize and accept it, or try to get into heaven by your own laurels. Now that would be lame.

Call Christianity a crutch. I like to think of it as being smart enough to realize that we are all lame and that our efforts are futile when we try to do anything without the supernatural power offered to us through the Holy Spirit. It indwells us all and helps us to recognize our lameness. If you don't think you're lame, just ask someone who knows you really well to give you an honest answer. Maybe you'll recognize the futility of your life without a being greater than yourself and will cry out for something much stronger than a crutch. I hope you never have to go through a tragedy without a "prop" (Dictionary.com: "Rigid support").

Lord, I thank You that my brother and sister-in-law have You in their lives to help them walk through this living nightmare. I thank You that they aren't too stubborn or prideful to realize that they would most likely have been put into a padded room without your intervention in their lives. I thank You that they are willing to share with others how they are leaning on You as they learn to walk again.

#LostbutFound

Suppose one of you has a hundred sheep and loses one of them. Does he not leave the ninety-nine in the open country and go after the lost sheep until he finds it? And when he finds it, he joyfully puts it on his shoulders and goes home. Then he calls his friends and neighbors together and says, "Rejoice with me; I have found my lost sheep." I tell you that in the same way there will be more rejoicing in heaven over one sinner who repents than over ninety-nine who do not need to repent.

—Luke 15:4 (NIV)

It seems that I am misplacing things more than usual lately— either that or my memory isn't quite what it used to be. Whatever the reason, my running list of lost items over the past month has grown.

It started with a pair of diamond earrings, something I'd splurged on for myself after many years. Knowing these weren't just ten-dollar earrings, that their value was great, had me searching high and low for them. About the same time, a friend of mine had picked me up to go out for lunch and run a couple of errands. When I got home, I realized that I was missing my spare key, which I knew I'd had in my possession before leaving the house. This key wasn't just the basic type that you can have made at your local home improvement store. This was the dealership type of key that is costly to replace. My list of "missing in action" was growing, and I found it quite disturbing. My friend who had picked me up had just told me that she was missing her good pair of reading glasses. Lost items seemed to be the theme of the day! Knowing that God cares about even the smallest details of our lives, we prayed together that we could locate some of these items and then went on with our day.

In an effort to locate these two items, I started dumping everything out of my jewelry chest and reorganizing dressers and moving them to search behind them. I called the restaurant where we had eaten, to ask them to search the booth, and did everything else I could think of to find them. I was determined I wouldn't rest until they were found. Everything on my to-do list took second place. My friend and I commiserated that we felt as if we were losing our minds!

I was reminded of the parable of the lost coin that Jesus shared in Luke 15:8–10 (NIV): "Suppose a woman has ten silver coins [footnotes say he was speaking of ten Greek drachmas, each worth about a day's wages] and loses one. Does she not light a lamp, sweep the house and search carefully until she finds it? And when she finds it, she calls her friends and neighbors together and says, 'Rejoice with me; I have found my lost coin.' In the same way, I tell you, there is rejoicing in the presence of the angels of God over one sinner who repents."

I love Jesus's parables because they are stories that we as humans can really relate to. We have all lost things of value. Jesus wanted us to understand how important people are to Him, especially those who are floundering on their own. He will never give up until He finds them! And when they are found, there will be much rejoicing!

Well, I found my earrings—and my keys, too. I'd left the earrings at a location we had visited, and my keys were in my friend's vehicle. As for her glasses, she found them in a drawer with her computer cords. And yes, we both rejoiced that what was lost had been found, encouraging us and reminding us that those loved ones in our lives who are lost are not beyond the reach of God. He is about the business of searching for and finding His own.

Thank You, Lord for never giving up on me and searching tirelessly for me, a lost sheep, and bringing me home to the fold.

#PerfectJustice

> Consider it pure joy, my brothers, whenever you
> face trials of many kinds, because you know that
> the testing of your faith develops perseverance.
> Perseverance must finish its work so that you may
> be mature and complete, not lacking anything.
>
> —James 1:2–4 (NIV)

I clearly remember the day our son called to tell me that he had been in a serious automobile accident, and the passenger in the other vehicle had been critically injured. Those injuries ultimately took his life.

I called my husband and our eldest son, and while I didn't know the details, I knew that a person was struggling for his life, so I made calls to family and friends to ask for prayer support.

The details of the accident started slowly coming as our son gave his account. He had been headed home from work, eastbound on a two-lane highway, in light rain, when an oncoming vehicle had made a left-hand turn right in front of his work truck. He explained how he hadn't even had time to brake until the vehicle was right in front of his line of sight.

He described how the driver of the car had fled the scene and how he had run to check on the passenger, who had taken the biggest impact. He explained that a girl who was working near the accident had run out, and they had both checked on the passenger with the life-threatening injuries. He said that when he saw the severity of his injuries, he told the girl that they needed to pray for this man while they waited for rescue personnel to arrive.

We later discovered that the man driving the car that had turned in front of our son was unlicensed. He had been driving a car that wasn't his, and he was not a US citizen. The man fled the scene but was later captured.

Our son, who was complaining of some hip pain, was taken to the hospital for x-rays. He had sustained some bruises but no breaks. His wounds were mostly emotional; he was visibly shaken by the fact that a man might lose his life after being hit by his truck—even though it was quite clear to him and the police that there would not have been any way to avoid this accident. There were no citations issued against our son, and blood samples were taken to clear him of any drug or alcohol use.

The accident was devastating to our son. Upon learning that the passenger had died, he was so upset that he dropped his college classes and moved to another state to work with some friends.

We later learned that a $3.5-million law suit was being filed against our son and the company that he was working for at the time. It was so difficult to believe this, knowing the facts. The driver of the other vehicle had failed to yield to the right of way, making a left hand turn right in front of the path of our son's truck; he had fled the scene but been captured later; he had pled guilty to negligence, spent three years in jail, and been deported to his country of origin. Now they were filing a law suit!

Not wanting our children to have the mentality that they had to be compensated for accidents, we didn't encourage a counter suit, although if there was ever a case for one, this would have been it.

The trial was finally scheduled three years and three months following the accident. Our son, who had been on his own for a couple of years, didn't really want us to be there, but we wanted to walk through this difficult time with him, and we suggested he discuss it with the attorneys representing him. In the end, he did agree to let us be present.

We sat and watched the entire jury selection process the morning of the trial. We heard all the questions asked by the lawyers of the jurors to determine experiences and opinions that might influence their decisions.

The jury selected, we watched each side jockey in front of the judge for their right to submit what they wanted the jury to observe and hear. Knowing many of the details of the case, I was taken aback by the amount of information pertaining to the case that was deemed inadmissible. This included our son praying with another witness over the passenger, details of another truck that had pulled out of the driveway before the victim's car made the turn—which would have explained why the driver pulled out—the fleeing of the scene that was turned into him running to get help (although we knew that he was hiding and that it took many police officers hours to find him). All were deleted from testimony, inadmissible. I watched and listened to all the "evidence," the witness depositions, and live witnesses. It was difficult to listen to accusations being made against our son when I believed so strongly that the other driver was the only person negligent in this accident.

We listened as the prosecuting attorneys tried to imply that our son was in some way negligent and therefore financially responsible to the family that had been left behind. It was difficult to sit and listen to the untruths spouted as if they were fact, but we continued day after day to sit there quietly and pray without ceasing that the truth would reign.

The final day of the trial came. Final statements were made, and the jury was sent out late in the day. My husband and I decided to wait for the jury's return, no matter how long it took. The jury had several options of degrees of negligence. After they had walked back into the courtroom, their representative announced, "We find the defendant and his company ... zero percent negligent."

We were so thankful that the jurors had seen through what was happening. We were glad for our son's sake, as he'd had to experience pain and suffering himself due to the actions of that other driver. We were happy that he'd been able to hear from a panel of jurors that he was innocent. We thought that it would help him to move on with his life after such a traumatic experience. Today we got a small glimpse of what Christ experienced, being falsely accused while innocent. The amazing part is that Christ quietly and willingly took on the punishment *we* deserved, so we—the guilty—could be completely exonerated! Now, that is good news!

This particular son had a favorite T-shirt that he wore in high school. On the front it had a line from Forrest Gump: "Ah'm not a smart man, but ah know what love is."

On the back it said, "Jesus Christ and Him crucified … and that's all ah have to say about that."

Dear Lord, thank You for walking with our son and us through this trial. I thank You that truth did reign today. We pray, too, for the family that lost their son and husband and daddy in this tragic accident. We pray that You will comfort them. We pray also for the driver of the car, who is living with the loss of life, that he will come to realize the forgiveness he has in in You.

#PerfectTiming

> While they were there, the time came for the baby
> to be born, and she gave birth to her firstborn, a son.
>
> —Luke 2:6–7 (NIV)

I was hurriedly preparing to leave to go help out our daughter and son-in-law, who were expecting their first child to be born at any moment. Knowing we would be away for almost three weeks, it was imperative that we paid some bills now, as we would be away on the dates that they were due. Our mortgage was due, and there wasn't enough to cover that. We needed to deposit money ASAP, but no monies were coming in.

My husband, who is self-employed, was waiting for money that was owed him. Having our own business requires patience, as we are dependent on clients paying us in a timely fashion.

I was feeling sorry for my husband, who was working so hard and yet not seeing the results of his labor. We talked about the desperation we were feeling and reminded each other of Gods faithfulness in providing. Then we went through our day, walking by faith, not by sight.

I got a call that afternoon from my son who works on tugboats. He had been doing another gig on some tourist boats while he awaited a call from a tug company. He was letting me know that his prayers had been answered. He had secured a job on a tug that was towing two naval ships to San Diego. He was being flown to Miami the very same afternoon. I gave thanks to God for providing for my son, and I continued my day.

My husband called after his morning appointments and informed me that he had found in the mailbox two checks that would take us through the month!

I stopped to praise God for His faithfulness in meeting our needs and the needs of our children. I confessed the waves of doubt that had come while we were waiting. I also thought of the Israelites, who had been waiting for their king to arrive for over two thousand years, and in particular the prophetess and widow Anna, who had come to the temple daily, praying and waiting to see the promise of a Messiah fulfilled in her lifetime. She had never doubted that what God had promised would come to pass.

Lord, thank You for Your provisions to us and for the reminder that the provisions come in Your perfect timing, including the birth of our Savior, who came at the "proper" time. As we wait for this grandchild to be born, we pray that she, too, will enter this world in Your perfect timing. We are in the dark about when that day and hour will be, but You know, and we wait in eager anticipation for Your perfect timing.

#ProppedUp

Trust in the Lord with all your heart and lean not on your own understanding; in all your ways submit to him, and he will make your paths straight.

—Proverbs 3:5–6 (NIV)

I spent a school year meeting weekly with a group of women to study what God's word had to say about prayer and praying together. The beauty of this group was that they were for the most part open books about their lives, sharing all their biggest struggles and concerns. Because of their authenticity, we had grown quite close.

I had walked through the year with a particular friend who was also part of this study, and I knew firsthand the hurts and disappointments she had been experiencing. As we were celebrating the coming summer break with a brunch, we decided to take a group picture. My friend, who had significantly withdrawn because of the pain she was experiencing, ambled up the steps that led to the stage. She leaned against the wooden pulpit, which was in the shape of a cross. I could tell she was just going through the motions that day. She was weary and literally just resting and waiting for everyone to gather. Then she turned around, saw the shape of the pulpit, and said to me in a lighthearted way, "I'm leaning on the cross!"

The words had no sooner left her lips than we both looked at each other, and we had an instant understanding. I think all I said was, "Yes, you are." Nothing more needed to be said. Those five little words that came out of her mouth had said it all. She was right where she needed to be. I immediately was reminded of the words to the hymn "Leaning on the Everlasting Arms."

What a fellowship, what a joy divine,
Leaning on the everlasting arms;
What a blessedness, what a peace is mine,
Leaning on the everlasting arms.

Leaning, leaning, safe and secure from all alarms;
Leaning, leaning, leaning on the everlasting arms.

What have I to dread, what have I to fear,
Leaning on the everlasting arms;

I have blessed peace with my Lord so near,
Leaning on the everlasting arms.

Leaning, leaning, safe and secure from all alarms;
Leaning, leaning, leaning on the everlasting arms.

—Lyrics by Elisha A Hoffman. Published in 1887

Lord, thank You for being the shoulder that we can lean on when our world is turned upside down. Only there will we find that safety, security, and peace that we long for.

#SummerofSuffering

Meanwhile, the moment we get tired in the waiting, God's Spirit is right alongside helping us along. If we don't know how or what to pray, it doesn't matter. He does our praying in and for us, making prayer out of our wordless sighs, our aching groans. He knows us far better than we know ourselves, knows our pregnant condition, and keeps us present before God. That's why we can be so sure that every detail in our lives of love for God is worked into something good.

—Romans 8:26–28 (MSG)

I hadn't even had time to think about what my summer was going to look like when my nineteen-year-old-son was in a serious car accident. I was told that the recovery time would be four to six months, so I knew the weeks ahead were determined for me.

My husband was next. He had a small accident in which he was ejected from a boat, breaking and bruising a couple of ribs. I don't know what his official injuries were, as he chose not to go to the doctor.

Forty-nine days had passed since our son's accident, when I

tripped over my vacuum cleaner cord. It wrapped itself around my middle left toe and, like a booby trap, yanked on it, dislocating and fracturing it in one swift tug. It came as a surprise to me that one little digit on my foot could cause my entire body to be pretty much functionless for a good week. Luckily, my son had given up his crutches just days before my mishap. I was just getting to the point where I could walk on the side of my foot and/or heel with not too much discomfort when *bam!* I clobbered it on the leg of a commode chair that my son was using in the shower during his recovery.

After two weeks of barely hobbling around, I decided to have my son's orthopedic surgeon take a look at it. After x-raying it, he realigned it. It hurt like crazy for a few seconds while he yanked on it, but I was amazed that when he was finished I could actually put my weight on my entire foot.

Reeling from all the paperwork and doctor and therapy appointments, we remembered that we had promised our youngest son that we would take care of his gynecomastia condition. In layman's terms, we'd promised him that we would see to it that his mini breast would be surgically removed.

As I was sitting in yet another doctor's office, this time in a breast-care center with my seventeen-year-old son, we started visiting with a man who was waiting with his mother-in-law. My son, who is very outgoing, plus he was excited that there was a member of the male species in the same room, noticed that his leg and shin were nicked, along with his toes. He asked him what had happened. The man explained that he had been unloading concrete boards with his son and that the boards had fallen on him. He said two of his toes had been broken and that his paramedic son had straightened them out at the scene. Immediately we were on common ground; his injury had happened just a day prior to mine. We exchanged our healing experiences and the fact that neither of us were yet brave enough to try on a shoe.

By the time we were called into the office, we had learned that he was a retired dentist and that he and his wife had two grown sons, who were now doing fine but had been through some things that had been hard on their parents. Their one son had been involved in a gun accident when he was a teen, and his whole mouth had had to be reconstructed. His other son had developed a brain tumor, which he overcame, and he shared how that trial had left them mentally exhausted. He was now in the process of caring for his parents and his wife's mother. His father-in-law had died not long ago, after a lengthy illness. Then his time was up at the doctor's. We shook hands with a mutual understanding of the toll that life can take on you. He had learned, as well, more about our family than I might have wished my son to share—like the BB-in-the-tongue story which I haven't shared. Now that I think of it, this man opened up and shared the story of his son's gun accident after my son had shared his personal experience.

Returning home, I dropped my son off so he could return to work, and I headed down the street to talk on my single-parent neighbor. The night before, her house had burned down, and I wanted to check on her. As we conversed, I said to her, "Don't you just wonder sometimes?" She responded that she didn't look at it that way. Yes, her house and all her belongings were gone, but she and her daughter were alive. That was a miracle, since the fire had started around midnight and the family dog had awakened their daughter around three in the morning.

There's something to be said about times of trouble. It's not like those times when things are going smoothly and life can almost become dull. You know in the middle of a tragedy that you have to do what you have to do. There is no doubt that God is smack dab in the middle of it, and there is purpose in it all. I reminded myself of the verse in Romans 8:28 (ESV): "All things work for the good for those who love God and are called according to His Purpose." I sometimes see how my mishaps are used and sometimes I don't. I do know, though, that while God doesn't cause all these events, He will take them and work them for our good.

A previous pastor of ours said he was asked all the time how there could be a loving God with all the evil in the world. His answer was, "Evil in the world? You bet! The greater question is, how can you live in this evil world *without* believing in a God that is greater than all this evil?"

Things were starting to smooth out that day, so I decided to take the rest of it for myself to play. I returned home to find my neighbor bringing the family dog to my door. The dog had a fishing lure—yes, a fishing lure—attached to her hindquarters! Even the dog had to participate in our summer of injuries!

Lord, thank You for the way you put people in our paths to help us all get through this life together. Thank You for reminding me, through my son, that if we are open and honest with others about our struggles they will be open with us about their lives. That way, we will all leave encouraged that we aren't alone in our sufferings in this world.

#TearsAreOkay

For the Lamb at the center of the throne will be their shepherd; "he will lead them to springs of living water." "And God will wipe away every tear from their eyes."

—Revelation 7:17 (NIV)

I was walking and at the same time catching up with a friend on the phone. She was sharing with me how she had run into an acquaintance at the grocery store and the floodgate of tears had opened. This woman had started sharing how her husband had left her after thirty-five plus years of marriage. My friend had gone through the same situation over six years earlier, so she could certainly understand the grieving process her friend was just beginning. I'm certain it was no coincidence; she was meant to cross paths with her that day.

As I was listening, I told her that I might need to call her back. I had spotted a woman I often saw along my walking path, and there was a good possibility she would want to talk.

I'd barely got the sentence off my lips that I would call her back when the woman called, "Is that you, Judy?" She went on, "I'm so glad I ran into you this morning. I felt so stupid the last time that I ran into you, and we talked and I cried. You must have thought I was crazy." I assured her that I had not thought that she was crazy and that I didn't understand why she was apologizing for her tears. She continued, "I just don't know what's wrong with me. All I do is cry."

She expounded about how she was going through a tough family situation and how she had been turning to a "friend" that she had known for years to share her burden with. She explained that the friend had told her not to call her anymore. She'd been devastated. "I know I probably talked too much about the situation, but don't you think that if she was a friend like I thought she was that she would have listened and tried to understand? I would have been there for her. Maybe she was using me." She continued, "My daughter reminded me that I was living in South Florida and maybe this woman just wanted a place to stay. Maybe she never really cared about me." Her mind was just reeling. I concurred that friends do let us down and shared that I had experienced that kind of hurt. But I reminded her that our true friend, Jesus, never tires of listening to us and is delighted when we bring all of our burdens to him. Her eyes started to fill up with tears again. "There I go again! What's wrong with me?"

I told her that nothing was wrong with her. I explained that my husband had been talking about how easily he cries now, more than anytime throughout his life. I told her that maybe it's that, as we get older, we have been through so much that we really come to a clearer understanding of how this really isn't our home. Maybe we long, as we have never before, to go home! She agreed. "Maybe that is it!"

Lord, thank You for creating tears. Forgive us for apologizing for them. Help us to be reminded that You created tear ducts as part of Your magnificent plan. Thanks for the reminder today that our citizenship isn't here but in heaven. The tears come because we know things are not as they should be, and the pain and hurt can be so overwhelming. We long for our Savior, who will one day bring everything under His control and transform our weary bodies into glorious ones!

CHAPTER 6

A LITTLE PERSPECTIVE

#Don'tJudgebyCover

As for those who seemed to be important ...
whatever they were makes no difference to me; God
does not judge by external appearance.

—Galatians 2:6 (NIV)

I was joining a group of people who were waiting for their numbers to be called at an event at a hotel. I grabbed a chair on the covered pool deck area, which was beautifully landscaped and manicured. As I waited, I couldn't help but listen to the conversations going on around me. I heard one lady tell her husband, "It is really pretty out here. I never would have guessed that, because from the front this place looks like nothing."

Looks like nothing. I wondered how many opportunities to get to know some beautiful people had been missed, by myself and others, because we had with a glance made a determination that the individual was not worth our time.

Living in a culture where beauty is determined by the physical, ad nauseam, I thought to myself how it works both ways. We can observe the outside and, with whatever demented scale we use, decide that a person is beautiful. But once we get to know the person, the result may be much different. On the other hand, we might get to know someone with reluctance, because they don't fit our demented idea of beauty, and be pleasantly surprised when we learn that he or she is quite beautiful.

When my four children were growing up, I tried to tell them that beauty isn't determined by what we see on the outside. I think some dating experiences had shown them that just because a girl or boy looks, in their judgment, great on the outside, that isn't necessarily an indicator that they would make the best partner for life. The argument they've given me is that you have to be attracted to a partner. I get that, but there is so much more to be attracted to than the outside appearance. It isn't just women who struggle with these issues. As a mom of three boys, I remember well the comments from other moms about the sizes of their sons. "He is really short for his age! My son is the same age but is so much taller." I tried so hard to let my boys know that it wasn't their size but their hearts that mattered. I loved the children's song, "Only a Boy Named David," by written by Arthur Arnott. Find it at hymnary.org.

Only a boy named David,
Only a little sling;
Only a boy named David,
But he could pray and sing.
Only a boy named David,
Only a rippling brook;
Only a boy named David,
But five little stones he took.

And one little stone went in the sling,
And the sling went round and round;
And one little stone went in the sling,
And the sling went round and round.
And round and round,
And round and round,
And round and round and round;
And one little stone went up in the air,
And the giant came tumbling down.

I have heard comments from adult men who have experienced feeling less of a man because of their stature. It breaks my heart, and I know it breaks the heart of God.

Jesus spoke harshly to religious leaders who worked really hard at looking good on the outside. "Woe to you, teachers of the law and Pharisees, you hypocrites! You are like whitewashed tombs, which look beautiful on the outside but on the inside are full of dead men's bones and everything unclean. In the same way, on the outside you appear to people as righteous but on the inside you are full of hypocrisy and wickedness" (Matthew 23:27–28 NIV).

When the Lord told Samuel to go to Jesse of Bethlehem, where He would show Samuel who He planned on appointing as king, Samuel incorrectly guessed a couple of times which one the Lord had chosen. But the Lord said to Samuel, "Do not consider his appearance or his height, for I have rejected him. The Lord does not look at the things man looks at. Man looks at the outward appearance, but the Lord looks at the heart" (1 Samuel 16:7 NIV).

After seven of the sons had passed, Samuel asked Jesse whether all of his sons were there. "There remains the youngest, but behold, he is keeping the sheep." And Samuel said to Jesse, "Send and get him, for we will not sit down till he comes here" (1 Samuel 16: 11).

Lord, in a culture inundated with people afraid to grow old, to be too tall, too short, too fat, too skinny, too ugly, or too small breasted, give us Your heart, so we can be content with what we have. Help us come to the understanding that these bodies we have are only temporary and that what we look like has absolutely nothing to do with our significance or how you see us.

Lord, give me the wisdom to know how to live in this culture for the remaining days of life. Let me be undaunted by what media, other people, and maybe even those closest to me have to say about things that You don't give a second thought about. Give me the ability to forgive and love those who have bought into what our culture has focused on as important.

#ElevatorMusic

Remember, our Message is not about ourselves;
we're proclaiming Jesus Christ, the Master. All we
are is messengers, errand runners from Jesus for you.
It started when God said, "Light up the darkness!"
and our lives filled up with light as we saw and
understood God in the face of Christ, all bright
and beautiful.

—2 Corinthians 4:5–6 (MSG)

It was just an ordinary elevator ride on the cruise ship we were on, with my husband and our daughter, her husband, and our eleven-month-old granddaughter.

But the ordinary turned into quite an unordinary moment, as my granddaughter decided to look at everyone individually on the elevator, cranking her head all around to smile at them and practice her newly learned wave and clap.

Her infectious smile and wave had several people talking to her, and when she turned to execute her clap, I couldn't believe the reaction that followed. She had the entire elevator simultaneously clapping along with her, which brought a huge smile to her already joyful little face! It was a happy moment for everyone on that elevator, and she had created it with her winsome smile and pleasant demeanor, by simply noticing others and making eye contact with them.

Her outgoing personality can be exhausting at times for our daughter, who isn't quite as much of an extrovert. This type of personality can be difficult to calm down if there is anyone around or any noise at all; she is afraid she will miss an opportunity to see what is going on or to greet someone.

The last night of our cruise she woke up crying. She was having difficulty staying asleep, as she was congested, and when she lay down it would drain, which made her cough. Hearing her cry and knowing that it was 2 a.m. and her parents had a long drive ahead of them the next day, my husband and I offered to take her for a stroll, in an effort to calm her down and see if we could get her to sleep. My daughter had told us about a swing on the ship that she'd enjoyed, so we located that. She fairly quickly calmed down, closed her little eyes, and went to sleep for quite a while. There was no one around at that time of morning—until the nighttime cleaning man came to empty the trashcan that was close to the swing. As soon as she heard the banging, her head popped up, and she proceeded to watch everything he was doing. She made her noise to greet a newfound friend, hoping and waiting for him to turn his attention to her, so she could perform her repertoire of smile and wave and clap.

As soon as the man finished and walked out of the area, without noticing her, her head dropped onto my shoulder, and she was asleep almost immediately. I couldn't help but think how we could learn from this precious little one. She was so focused on others that she would forfeit what she needed most, whether it be food or sleep, to make sure she could smile at anyone within her line of vision and encourage them in a way I doubt she even realized she was capable of doing.

As we age, our smiles don't come quite so easily. We put on our game faces to get through all that the world demands. Especially in an elevator, people will go to great lengths to avoid eye contact. It is just too close to their personal space, and people find it uncomfortable. Well, it sure didn't make the people that we were in the elevator with uncomfortable.

I'm going to try to emulate my granddaughter by using my facial muscles a lot more. Maybe not by waving—my wave isn't nearly as cute as hers—but by smiling and saying hello or initiating a short conversation. Hopefully this will bring a bit of joy to the day of someone who has crossed my path.

Lord, thank You for grandchildren and the uninhibited natural joy that they share with all those around them. Help me to exude that joy, which comes from the hope I have that, no matter what my age or circumstances, strangers will see a bright and beautiful shining from Your love inside of me.

#FridaytheThirteenth

Before I formed you in the womb I knew you, before you were born I set you apart.

—Jeremiah 1:5 (NIV)

It was Friday, July 13, 2001. I was leaving that afternoon for a Women of Faith conference, and I was leisurely washing and ironing my clothes in preparation for the weekend.

When I was ready to leave to pick up a friend, some medication for my father-in-law arrived in the mail. I decided it would be nice to save my husband a trip by dropping it off at his dad's retirement home.

As I drove there, was listening to the radio, I heard jokes about Friday the thirteenth and the superstitions associated with it. In my mind I scoffed at the jokes.

When I arrived, there was a full-blown party in progress. Waiters were passing out party punch in champagne glasses, and lots of people were dancing. I decided to see if I could inconspicuously walk through the crowd to the door that led to the nurses' station. But who did I see standing right in my path but my father-in-law. Upon seeing me, he grabbed me and started dancing with me. I dropped my keys, and as he picked them up, I looked for a side table to empty my hands so that I could dance.

We danced a couple of dances and sang along with "He's got the whole world in His hands." It was a festive time, and it was uplifting to see those men and women, many of whom could barely walk, recalling tunes and "strutting their stuff!"

After a few dances, I told Dad that I would have to be leaving. When I was a little way down the road, my phone rang. It was my eldest son, and he said, "Hey, Grandma!" It was my first grandchild! It had been due around the eighteenth of July, and I hadn't expected that early an arrival. I had been dancing at the moment of my first grandchild's birth! God is so good. I hadn't planned to stop there and would not have if the medicine hadn't arrived at that very time, that very day, that very hour.

People would call that coincidence. I call it a God who loves me and my granddaughter so much that he wanted me to celebrate by dancing at the very moment that she was coming into this world! I continued on to pick up the friends whom I was going with, and the celebration continued throughout the evening as we ate out together and they called me Grandma all night.

A date associated with much darkness was one of the happiest days of my life! I ain't afraid of no ghosts!

Lord, I thank You that you are such a God of detail and that I don't have to worry about any superstitions with You at the helm of my life. Thank You for seeing to it that I was literally dancing, one of my favorite things to be doing, when my first grandchild was being born!

#Intruder

> But you, man of God, flee from all this, and pursue righteousness, godliness, faith, love, endurance and gentleness. Fight the good fight of the faith.
>
> —1 Timothy 6:11–12 (NIV)

We have a blue land crab phenomenon in the area where we live. Every August and September, during their mating season, they descend on us and appear all over the road, in the yards, and in our pools. If you leave a door to your house open, there is a good chance you will at some point have an unwanted visitor.

I was busy cleaning away on a Saturday morning, when I went from my office area into my kitchen area, and there I saw it. My garage door was cracked open, and this land crab was defiantly looking at me as he stood in my kitchen!

I immediately stared him down, and as I did, he raised both of his ugly pincher-like claws, letting me know that he was going to defend his right to be there.

I knew this meant war, and although I don't have claws, I was determined to get this unwanted creature out of my house. My usual course of action would have been to call my husband, but he was at work, and I thought I could handle this.

I quickly went to the garage, keeping my eye on him the whole time, because I knew he would retreat. He scurried under my tea cart, thinking that he would be safe. I found a shoe box in the garage, which I grabbed and flung over him. Then I scooped him up with the lid and cautiously closed it over his ugly little head. Success!

I started thinking: what other intruders have we allowed in our homes that aren't quite so quickly recognizable? Could one be a book, a video game, a TV show, or an Internet site that takes up a lot of our time and energy?

How often do we ensnare ourselves in either activities or thoughts that complicate our lives, robbing us of peace-filled days that could be the norm rather than the exception? Wouldn't it be great if we would commit to avoiding these activities or thoughts that could be harmful to us or our family members with as much energy as I used in going after that unwanted intruder?

Dear Lord, we need You; every minute we need You. Help us to hold our thoughts captive so that they align with the truth of Your word. Thank You for loving us so much that You remind us through the Holy Spirit of things that are unhealthy for us and steer us away from whatever is keeping us from Your best for us!

#MadeforPurpose

For we are God's workmanship, created in Christ
Jesus to do good works, which God prepared in
advance for us to do.

—Ephesians 2:10 (NIV)

My husband and I were having a productive day getting ready
for a visit from my mother and a friend of hers. They were planning
to swing by on their way to another destination. While I continued
scurrying around, my husband, who was starting to get hungry,
offered to sauté the vegetables for a veggie wrap I had planned for
our lunch.

As I came around the corner to enter the kitchen, I saw him bent
over, cleaning a quarter of the veggies off the kitchen floor, which
was in need of a good scrubbing. Hoping he wasn't going to try and
salvage them, I asked him what had happened. He explained, "Well,
I learned that you can't flip things in a square pan like you can in a
round pan." He was famous for his omelet making and, after years,
had mastered the art of flipping the omelet over. He had tried it
with the veggies in a square pan, and it had resulted in a huge mess.

I love good cookware; it makes such a difference in cooking
and cleanup. We are at the stage of life where we will spend a little
extra for the good pans. One place where my husband really enjoys
shopping is a kitchen store. It is amazing to look at all the different
shapes and sizes of pans, each with a specific purpose. There is the
perfect omelet pan; there is the round pan with higher sides for
stir fries; and my most recent favorite pan is a pan to grill fish and
veggies. It has ridges, and it sautés veggies beautifully, similar to
how they turn out if you grill them on a backyard grill. While you
can use some pans for purposes other than what they are made for,
the result won't be the best possible outcome, because you are using
them for something they were not designed for.

People are the same way. They were designed by our Creator with different gifts and abilities, to be used in different ways so that God can be glorified.

It is when we try to do things that we are not designed for that we make big messes of things. In a small-group setting, where you really get to know each other well, it becomes clear which gifts are in the group when you spend time with each other and listen to each other's passions. In our present small group, we have quite a variety. We have one woman who loves to study scripture and teach what she has learned to small gatherings. There is another woman who, while an introvert, quietly encourages others in ways that she doesn't even realize. I personally have been on the receiving end of a gift of encouragement from her. Another woman has the gift of giving; she will on occasion treat others to lunch or offer to purchase a new Bible or book for someone. We have one woman who has the gift of evangelism; she is eager to talk to any strangers she might run into and encourage them in their walk with God.

We have men in the group who bring the gift of service. Nothing makes them feel more encouraged in themselves than being able to offer their maintenance skills to help others. Another man in our group listens and will often share insight from his life experiences that presents another way of looking at things. There is still another man who is detailed oriented and a good leader.

Just as it was with the square pan, if you took these people and had them operating in capacities other than with their own gifts, it would be unfair to them. They would be miserable, and others would suffer, as they would not be participating in works that were prepared in advance for them. They would not be doing what they were designed for. That, like my husband's veggies, would end in a big mess.

Lord, thank You for the way You have gifted me. Help me to use these gifts to encourage those around me who may benefit from my unique gifts. Let not a day go by when I am not willing to do the work that You have prepared in advance for me to do. For it is right in the middle of doing what You have called me to do that I will find my deepest cravings satisfied.

#MoreThanaJob

Work willingly at whatever you do, as though you
were working for the Lord rather than for people.

—Colossians 3:23 (NLT)

A commentator who was covering the rescue of the Chilean mine workers in October of 2010 asked the rescue workers how they were doing as they tirelessly went about digging out the thirty-three miners through the day and night. One of the rescuers responded with, "It's hard to think about time when you are saving lives."

What a perspective. Can you imagine what a different world it would be if we would individually wake up asking God to use each and every day as He desires, with the gifts he has uniquely created us with?

I found myself doing some caregiving for a couple who had been married for sixty-five years. The husband had had to go into a rehab situation, and so I was taking his wife several times a week to visit him.

Concerned that her husband of all those years was getting good care, she was noticing differences in the quality of his care. Some of the nurses and aides were very kind and their countenances very pleasant; it was all over their faces. Others were, as she described it, doing their jobs almost robotically, with expressionless faces. It was obviously just a job to them rather than a calling, and it was affecting the care that the patients were receiving.

It doesn't matter whether you are a volunteer, a paid employee, a wife, or a mother. We all have callings on our lives. If we were to start each day working out of gratitude that the Lord has given us breath for one more day and work for Him rather than working for the approval of our bosses or other men or women, the world could be changed!

Lord, thank You for the way You have uniquely gifted each one of us. Help us to know Your desires for us on a daily basis, and when the opportunity comes for us to throw a life raft to someone who is sinking, help us to recognize it and offer what we can.

#NoPower

> You see, at just the right time, when we were still "powerless," Christ died for the ungodly. Very rarely will anyone die for a righteous man, though for a good man someone might possibly dare to die. But God demonstrates His own love for us in this: While we were still sinners, Christ died for us.
>
> —Romans 5:6 (NIV)

A busy week ended with a rainstorm, and I was looking forward to running errands and then curling up with a "blankie" in my favorite recliner, while catching up on testimony from a highly publicized trial that had me captivated. I returned home to discover that my cable was out—which meant no television, no home phones, and no Internet!

I tried the twenty-four-hour number for my cable company and attempted the reboot method to no avail. Then I received a text from a friend, who asked whether I was watching the trial, as it was taking some interesting turns. "No," I angrily texted back, "We have no cable service!" She quickly asked if I wanted to come join her. I couldn't get there quickly enough!

I was surprised at how I had become "unglued" about not being able to watch TV or get on the Internet. I had noticed how addicted "others" were—but I hadn't put myself in that category! I decided I would try the next morning to get this situation fixed, and I became even more agitated when they told me they couldn't come out until the Tuesday morning. That meant four nights and four and a half days of no service! By now I was talking—okay, ranting—about how we had lived through hurricane force winds before and hadn't lost cable. It was then that my logical, long-suffering husband, who could take or leave the television, kindly said to me, "Honey, did you stop and think that maybe someone has hit a power pole and a bad accident has caused this situation?" His comment stopped me in my selfish tracks.

Someone could be out there suffering at that moment, and all I could do was complain about how my comfy lifestyle was being affected. Wow. Okay, it was time to put things in perspective. Sometimes we just need a wake-up call. I started wondering how I could have gotten so far off track from what was important.

I have heard before that busyness can be a tool of the enemy. That's when we don't take the time to slow down and hear that small, still voice, the voice of our Creator. My reaction to this situation was a warning to me that perhaps I had bought into some things of the world that were distracting me from my time alone with God. I then thought about the fact that when we are so busy we miss the power that is available to us through the Holy Spirit. *No power!* We are so busy checking e-mails, watching television, texting messages, checking social networks, making phone calls, and googling that we have very little time to connect with the One who desires for us to be still and connect with Him. Even though we need to know how to do a lot of these things to live in today's world, we don't have to let it have that kind of power over us.

Lord, forgive me for being so selfish. Lord, I am thinking of this person on trial for what the world is describing as an unthinkable crime. I know I am every bit as capable of unthinkable acts. I see how quickly my heart can turn from You when I find my comforts being taken away from me. Lord, I need You every step of the way to do Your work in me and through me; only then will I have power that can never be shut off. Thank You for loving me when I am lovable, but even more, thank You for loving me when I am unlovable. Thank You for using my weaknesses to plug me into the greatest power source available.

#OneMoreDay

A father to the fatherless, a defender of widows, is God in his holy dwelling. God sets the lonely in families, he leads forth the prisoners with singing; but the rebellious live in a sun-scorched land.

—Psalm 68:5–6 (NIV)

When I arrived on Memorial Day at the home of the elderly lady whom I help, I walked into her bedroom, as I always do, with my *yoo-hoo!* and she responded with the same greeting! She had been listening to her AM radio station, where she catches the morning news, and she started to share with me about a song she had just listened to. As I started helping her put on her support stockings, she continued. "I couldn't understand all the words, but it was about "If I could have just one more day." Knowing that her husband was ninety-three and in a rehab facility, I thought maybe she was being sentimental about him not being home for Memorial Day.

I left her to go start her breakfast. I was planning oatmeal topped with some blueberries and strawberries to brighten her day for Memorial Day. While she was eating, I told her that I could look up the song on my phone and play it, and so I did. I googled "One More Day" and discovered that it was the title of a Diamond Rio song. She affirmed that it was the song she had heard, and we both teared up as we listened to it together this time.

I cleaned up her breakfast dishes, and she asked if we could get some bills out that were on her mind. She also wanted to send a check to one of her children, along with a note. She handed me the note after she had written it and asked me to read it. In it she had expressed to her daughter that she was remembering her daughter's grandfather today, which was her own dad. She had recently shared with me that she'd lost her daddy when she was only fifteen years old. She went on to tell her daughter that her life as a fifteen-year-old had been forever changed as of that day. As she was writing the check for her daughter, she asked me what the date was. When I told her, she peered up at me with a look of disbelief. "Really?" She then explained that this was the actual date that she had lost her dad, and her tears began to flow. I then understood why the song had affected her so much this day. One more day with her daddy was what she wished for. We had a good cry together, and then we moved on to the task at hand for the day, preparing to visit her husband at the rehab center.

We arrived at the rehab, gave him some treats, and wished him a happy Memorial Day. Knowing he had been in the Air Force, I looked up the Air Force song on my phone so I could play it for him. As I was holding it to his ear so he could hear it, I heard his bride sniffling. I knew he was hard of hearing but figured he would at least enjoy watching the video on YouTube of the planes taking off. He did indeed, and he responded with, "They aren't doing anything I can't do!"

Just after that, another man was being wheeled outside on a stretcher for some fresh air. My friend looked at me, and we both had the same thought at the same time. We had talked to this man before about being in the Marine Corps, as he had been wearing a polo with the Marine Corps emblem. She asked me if I could find the Marine Corps song for him, and I said I could. I followed him outside, where I thanked him for serving our country and asked him if he would like to hear the corps song and watch the video. He took the phone from my hand and listened and watched. When it was finished he thanked me.

We both were a bit disappointed that the facility hadn't decorated a bit more for this special day, that there was no American flag on display. But there was an understanding between us that this had been quite a special Memorial Day for us, because we had tried to brighten the day of a couple of veterans. She had exemplified what my grandmother had taught me: when you're feeling sorry for yourself, do something for someone else!

Thank You, Lord, for a fun, meaningful day. Thank You for protecting and providing for my friend and her mom when they lost their husband and daddy that day many years ago. Thank You for the faith my friend placed in You, and thanks for the country that we live in, not by our choosing but by Your sovereignty.

#OrdainedWait

Wait for the Lord; be strong and take heart and wait for the Lord.

—Psalm 27:14 (NIV)

I have learned that in those times when I have to wait, I have a choice. I can choose to either think negative thoughts about how this is messing up my day or I can just rest and wait to see if there is a larger purpose in my waiting.

Today was one of those days. I was seated for what promised to be a long wait, and a woman sitting at a nearby table invited me to join her. We were just exchanging small talk when I mentioned to her that she looked familiar to me. She told me that she worked part time at a local grocery where I shopped, and we decided that that must be where I had seen her. As we were talking, she continued, with tears welling up in her eyes, "My daughter just died six weeks ago." Glancing down at her watch, she informed me, "It will be six weeks ago in about ten minutes."

Wow! Ten minutes. This woman was grieving the loss of her forty-something-year-old daughter, and it was so fresh that even the time of her death was a painful reminder of how she was gone from this earth and her life. I thought, *Lord, show me how to comfort this woman whom you have so clearly put in my path.*

I expressed my sympathies and asked her how she was coping. She shared how her daughter had been struck by a serious disease when she was in her twenties and that it had gotten worse. She explained that her daughter's husband hadn't been able to handle it anymore and she had been taken to a nursing home close to her mom to be cared for. This woman was so thankful for the care the staff had given her child over the last twenty years, and you could tell she considered them family.

She recalled how her daughter had loved it when people from different churches in the area had come to the nursing home to sing at Christmas time. Her long-term memory had been able to recall all the familiar songs that she'd loved. The mother said it had been difficult for her, though, because her daughter had been unable to sing anymore, and people didn't understand. She'd found it difficult to watch people staring at her. She then shared with me about her grandchildren and how proud she was of them. She told me her daughter's children had decided to have a memorial at Christmas time because her daughter had so loved Christmas. They would all get together and sing her favorite Christmas songs together to honor her life. She was very excited about their plan.

I listened, and then our short time together was interrupted as my number was called. After taking care of my business, I sought her out and told her that I was glad we had been able to talk to each other. I told her that God would continue to comfort her. We exchanged smiles with a quiet understanding that we had connected on more than a superficial level.

Lord, forgive me for the times that I have complained about having to wait and, in my whiny selfishness, missed opportunities that You have provided to be a listening ear and possibly a vessel of encouragement to a hurting soul. Please fill this mom with peace today—the peace that only You can give, the peace that passes all human understanding.

#PowerofWrittenWord

For the word of God is living and active. Sharper than any double-edged sword, it penetrates even to dividing soul and spirit, joints and marrow; it judges the thoughts and attitudes of the heart.

—Hebrews 4:12 (NIV)

Once you're a mom, Mother's Day takes on a whole new meaning! As the years go by, the meaning of Mother's Day changes along with the changes your children are going through or have gone through.

Perhaps you can remember the first year of being a mom, and you have an understanding of the demanding side of motherhood. It is nice to be recognized.

As your child turns to a toddler and starts asserting his or her will, you have another perspective of all that being a mom means.

Then your children reach school age, and the busyness of motherhood begins: the car pools, the field trips, the homework.

Your children reach junior high, and it's boys and girls noticing each other. It's time to start talking about things you wish you could avoid talking about, but you know you have to.

When your children reach high school, the realization comes

that, in a short four years, their adult lives are about to begin. You have a brief window of guiding them.

Your children may choose to go to college or tech school or possibly enter the workplace, and this means it is time to say goodbye. It is a painful time for moms, and you realize that part of motherhood is letting go. It is a time of struggle.

When my children were at all different ages, my husband was so good about making it my special day. When the children were little, he stepped up the help with the baby or toddler, and when the children were school age, he helped them by fixing breakfast in bed for Mom. At junior-high time, he would let me be "queen of the day," and the children would serve me. This year we were taking my mom, who was alone for the first time on mother's day since my dad's death, to a historic hotel near her home. We went to church together and headed out. As I gave my name at the hotel, I looked up to see my oldest son and his wife and three children! What a fun surprise! My daughter, who I knew was wishing we could be together, called a couple of times, and my other son, who was at his girlfriend's college graduation, made an effort to call me. As we headed home after a special day, I checked my phone and found an e-mail that had come in from our third child, my second son, and this is what I read:

"Happy Mother's Day, Mom. Thanks for all of my good qualities! You're part of the reason I am who I am today! My cleanliness and cooking skills, also my people skills. All of these play key roles in my success as a mariner! Also, thanks for squeezing me out; that must have hurt! Son # 2"

I was struck by how much reading my son's words affected me. I cried as I read each letter of the e-mail, missing him and thinking of his thoughtfulness in remembering me. Perhaps that's why God left His words to us in written form—so that we could read them over and over, ponder and learn, and grow and give thanks.

Lord, thank You for leaving Your word for us. Thank You for its trustworthiness and power to change lives. Thank You for the pastors and for the Sunday school teachers, and for the missionaries, home and abroad. Thank You for the Bible study teachers, the women leaders who share God's word, and even the ordinary men or women who take the opportunity to share their faith with whoever you put in their path.

#PureJoy

He spoke the word that healed you, that pulled you back from the brink of death. So thank God for his marvelous love, for his miracle mercy to the children he loves; Offer thanksgiving sacrifices, tell the world what he's done—sing it out!

—Psalm 107:20–22 (MSG)

I was driving into a gated community to pick up a friend and was prepared to give my name and the name of the friend whom I was going to visit. I told her I was on the "list." It was the usual routine, but suddenly the usual became, well, anything but routine. It became an incredible, unexpected joyful moment!

The woman at the gate gave me my slip of paper for entry. Then she looked at me and said, "Can I tell you something?" I said sure, and she continued. "I went to the doctor today, not expecting very good news. You see, I am almost completely blind in one eye, and my sight is starting to come back!" I could tell that she was so filled with joy that she just couldn't keep it to herself!

I asked her if she had an eye condition that had caused the blindness, and she said, "No, I was beaten up and left for dead forty years ago." She continued, "But I lived!" She explained that she had been twenty-nine years old at the time and that she knew the person who had inflicted the injury. When I inquired where this had happened, she named my home state. We were on common ground immediately.

I listened as she continued with her story. "I'm just so thankful that it happened to me and not to an elderly person or a child."

Wow, what a perspective! I felt privileged that, with all the cars going through, she had picked me in mine to share her story with. Although, who knows, she might have spread her joy all day long!

Lord, thank You for Your children who are willing to shout for joy and tell of Your marvelous works and mercy shown to them. When Your people choose to keep the wonderful things You are doing in their lives to themselves, so many others are robbed of Your joy! Thanks for this woman whom you placed in my path today. I may never see her again on this earth, but we shared joy today. I don't know exactly how it will work, but I believe that when we are both in heaven we will somehow recognize each other and continue our "joy fest"!

#RoyalWedding

> While society has different classes based on economics, with God there is no distinction and no favoritism. "Rich and poor have this in common: The Lord is the Maker of them all."
>
> —Proverbs 22:2 (NIV)

My husband had a deadline approaching, and he awakened early one morning to go into work. As I considered rolling over to postpone my rising, I suddenly remembered that this was the day of the royal wedding between Prince William and Catherine (Kate) Middleton!

I was so excited to think that I was up in time to watch the wedding and could do so in the comfort of my bed! Almost every girl enjoys watching a wedding, and I am no exception. I fluffed my pillows and settled in to catch a glimpse of this grand historic event. My sweet husband even fixed me a cup of cappuccino to enjoy while I settled in for the extravaganza!

I flipped through the channels to hear the different angles from the myriad of commentators and was just enjoying the fact that I could actually focus on the details uninterrupted, something I hadn't been able to do for years, being a mom. I was watching history in the making, and I could do with no interruptions or commentaries from children!

I loved the verse that Kate's brother read out of the book of Romans concerning love. A commoner—or, as Webster's describes it, "A citizen not of the nobility"—was reading what God's word had to say about love, and he was doing it with enthusiasm, I might add. "Bless those who persecute you; bless and do not curse. Rejoice with those who rejoice; mourn with those who mourn, live in harmony with one another. Do not be proud, but be willing to associate with people of low position. Do not be conceited" Romans 12:14–16).

I kept hearing how Kate was handling her newfound fame with exceptional ease and poise "for a commoner" and suddenly I realized that her maiden name sounded quite familiar! While I was growing up in a blue-collar family (labeled by society a *commoner* myself) I suddenly recalled from my memory banks, I had gone to elementary and high school with a little girl who shared the same first and last name with this new duchess! I went to my high school yearbook, and sure enough, this classmate shared the same name but with a different spelling.

As I listened to God's word being spoken in the ceremony, I was pleased to hear it said aloud that all weddings are royal weddings. I thought of my daughter's recent wedding and those of the daughters of close friends and family. While very nice and quite common in comparison, these were every bit as important. Webster's definition of *importance* is "of great power." When God is asked to be part of a wedding ceremony, His power is present at the couple's union.

This was the last day as a commoner for Princess Kate Middleton, and it can be the last day as a commoner for anyone wishing to change his or her status from commoner to royalty.

I don't know whether my classmate or the duchess of England are trusting in the work of the Savior, Jesus Christ, but if they are, they are indeed royal, whatever their birthrights. "But you are a chosen people, a royal priesthood, a holy nation, God's special possession, that you may declare the praises of him who called you out of darkness into his wonderful light. Once you were not a people, but now you are the people of God; once you had not received mercy, but now you have received mercy" (1 Peter 2:9–10 NIV).

Dear Lord, thank You for showing me mercy and for declaring me innocent when I was guilty. Thank You for calling me out of darkness into Your wonderful light. Love, a daughter of the King.

#SayItOutLoud

But in your hearts revere Christ as Lord. Always be prepared to give an answer to everyone who asks you to give the reasons or the hope that you have. But do this with gentleness and respect.

—1 Peter 3:15 (NIV)

My daughter recently posted a picture of her daughter, my twenty-month-old granddaughter on her social network page. She was at a restaurant, sitting in a high chair and straining to turn her head to watch the people behind her. My daughter had added the comment, "Apparently she'd rather be eating dinner with the people behind us!"

I had to laugh, but I totally understand my granddaughter's personality. I don't want to scare my daughter, but she reminds me a lot of myself! I told my daughter that she is just a "people person" who seizes every opportunity to make a new friend. The only difference is she hasn't yet learned to be discreet about listening to people's conversations!

We recently stopped to get a bite to eat at a burger joint, and as I was seating myself, I saw these three friends walk in. I couldn't help but notice the shirt one of the girls was wearing. It was hot pink, with black letters that read, "Say It Out Loud!" I asked my husband if he thought it would be weird to ask her about her shirt. Yes, I had my head turned to look too! I have learned to ask my husband whether what I'm about to do might embarrass him or if he'd rather I'd focus on him. But the beauty of being married for over forty years is that he knows and loves me as I am. He said, "Go for it!'

So I approached the girl and told her that I'd noticed her shirt. I explained that I like to write about different things; would she mind if I asked her what the phrase on her shirt meant to her? She was younger than I'd thought, and she said, "I don't know, I just liked the shirt!"

We both laughed, and then I said, "Is it kind of like, 'Just say what you're thinking'?"

Her friend who was with her chimed in, "Yes, that's what it means—like, don't be chicken!" It was a short conversation, but I was glad I'd asked.

As I got up to leave, a male friend who was with them approached me and it crossed my mind that maybe I had gotten too personal with his friends and that he was going to tell me about it. To my relief and surprise, he started questioning me about writing. He explained that his friends had mentioned that I liked to write, and he went on to reveal that he was into writing inspirational poetry. Did I have any insight into how to go about getting things published? I explained to him that I was just starting the process myself and shared with him the little I did know.

I liked the message of the shirt. While we learn with age to discriminate which thoughts we share, it's scary to think about sharing all our thoughts. The other extreme is to be chicken about the things that matter the most.

I was glad I'd spoken to the girl. I was reminded in reading Psalms the following morning about sharing what God has done in our lives. "Oh, thank God—he's so good! His love never runs out. All of you set free by God, tell the world! Tell how he freed you from oppression, then rounded you up from all over the place, from the four winds, from the seven seas … Tell the world what he's done. Sing it out! (Psalm 107:1–3, 22 MSG).

Dear Lord, thank You for creating each of us with unique personalities and characteristics for Your special purpose! Give us wisdom as moms to know how to raise and encourage those personalities that are much different than ours as well as those that are just like ours! Help us to know that You gave us each of our children to raise, knowing that we were just the mom that you thought that child needed, and that we would both grow through all the good times and the bad into the persons that you desired us to be. Give us courage to share with others as the opportunities come our way, to not be chicken, and to "Say It Out Loud!"

#ShipsonFire

We can make our plans, but the Lord determines our steps.

—Proverbs 16:9 (NLT)

When our children were small, most of our family vacations revolved around natural springs and fishing. With our eldest out of the nest and two teens and a preteen at home, we decided it would be fun to plan a Caribbean cruise!

We had fun looking at all the excursions that we might like to take. The planning of the trip and the anticipation was every bit as enjoyable as the trip itself.

The starting day arrived in July of 1998, and we headed down to the port of Miami. We made it through all the long lines and check-ins and were finally on the ship, the *Ecstasy*! We took our luggage to our room and then headed to the deck to relax and prepare for the bon voyage celebration.

As the boat pulled away from the dock, my husband and the two boys were on the lower deck, near the engines, and my daughter and I had gone up to the next open deck to sit and watch from above. Our adventure was about to begin! As the ship slowly cruised its way out of the port, our youngest son noticed a bellow of smoke coming off the back of the ship. Was it diesel fuel? he asked his dad. My husband told him that he didn't think so, that it smelled like burning plastic.

Things moved quickly after that, as it became clear that the smoke exiting the back of the ship was anything but normal. My husband asked me to alert some of the crew. I immediately found a waiter and asked whether he was aware of the smoke. There was definitely a language barrier; most of the crew were Italian, and he came back to me carrying a Coke!

Soon after that, announcements started coming that there was, indeed, a fire on the ship but that it was under control. As the passengers waited and watched, the fire appeared to be getting worse. We could look over the side of the ship and see flames shooting through the windows. The passengers were getting scared.

I don't understand all that there is to maritime protocol, but apparently it is in the captain's best interest if he and his crew put the fire out. After some hours, it became frustrating; the coast guard was present, ready, and willing to put out the fire, but they had to wait for permission from the captain.

As we waited, everyone was summoned to their muster stations. Those exercises are often frustrating, as hundreds of people are packed into a small space for a drill, but this time it was different.

There was much confusion, and you could see fear in many eyes. Even the crew was a little panicky. My husband, the ultimate protector, told us that we would not be staying in this room. He feared that if it got worse we could literally be trampled by people, so we found a safe out-of-the-way corner on an upper deck and hung out as things unfolded. We noticed that there were several families that had made the same decision.

Our next objective was to try and secure some life vests, as they were scarce. They were in the rooms, and we weren't allowed to go to the rooms. The few that were on the decks had been taken. We finally got one for our youngest son. Many people went without. My children had always joked with me, when I would show off my floating ability, that it was because of the extra fat cells I had. Now we could still see the shoreline, and I told them that if we had to swim to shore, they would be thankful for my buoyancy, as it might save their lives. We were prepared to jump if it became necessary.

After what seemed like hours, the workers from the tugboats that were present in the port started fighting the fire. There were cheers as the passengers realized that help had finally arrived.

After hours of waiting and stress, it was confirmed that the ship would have to pulled back into port and that this cruise would not be taking place. Our one son, who had not been excited about the cruise in the first place, was excited that it wasn't going to happen, but the rest of us were disappointed.

They finally let us go back into our rooms; they had determined that it was safe enough for everyone to stay in their rooms for the night. But at 4 a.m. we were all awakened and told that the fire marshal had said everyone had to exit the ship. We were relieved that the ship had never made it out of the port; we heard later that if the ship had been out to sea there would not have been any way to fight the fire, and it would have resulted in many deaths.

I have learned through experiences like this that expectations will get me into trouble every time. We can (and we have to) make plans, but if we do it with no expectations, it is much more enjoyable for all.

I was again reminded of this adventure and the uncertainty of our lives when my neighbor recently knocked on my door to tell me he and his wife were back home. I thought he was there to share with me their incredible adventure. They had planned a trip of a lifetime, an eighteen-day river cruise to Europe.

The plan had been to go to four countries and multiple rivers. Their trip had involved driving hours up to the east coast to their departure airport. He told me how they'd arrived early, so they wouldn't have time stresses and would be able to just relax. When it got close to the time, they gathered their carry-on baggage and went up to the check-in, where the agent grabbed his wife's passport ripping one of the pages! They were then instructed to go to customs, as it was now an invalid passport!

They couldn't believe it when they were told that they could go into New York and get a new one. It was a Friday night, with the office closing at 5 p.m., and there was not enough time to get there through the Friday-night traffic in the city. Their trip of a lifetime wasn't going to happen, and they were hours away from their home.

Fortunately, they had family in the area whom they were able to stay with. But it seems things got worse. He had to go to the hospital twice for what they believed to be food poisoning. Wow—we really never know what a day will or will not bring! I really thought they handled the disappointment with a good attitude. As he said, at least no one died.

Dear Lord, We don't always understand why things happen the way they do, but we do know that You know the goings-on of our limited days on this earth. I am reminded that this life can end so abruptly. I am thankful to know that, whatever comes our way, if we trust in You, we can expect it to be a "bon voyage"!

#SnailMail

> For everything that was written in the past was
> written to teach us, so that through endurance and
> the encouragement of the Scriptures we might have
> hope.

—Romans 15:4 (NIV)

A friend of mine shared with me a conversation she recently had with her mail carrier. Upon greeting the carrier, she told her, "I hope you brought something besides credit card applications and bills."

Upon hearing this, the carrier asked her, "What would you want?"

She replied, "An encouraging note would be nice."

The woman then asked my friend, "When was the last time you mailed out a note to someone?" Then she added, "You've got to send them out to receive them!"

My friend, in sharing this conversation with me, said, "I guess she told me!" We laughed, and both of us felt encouraged that in this high-tech world the "outdated" art of letter writing still had a place. It might even have a higher place, as the techie stuff is making our busy world less and less personal. We decided that as long as we were breathing we would do our part to continue the writing, in hopes of encouraging those we encounter along the journey of life.

I have a box in my bedroom where I keep notes and letters have been an encouragement to me throughout my life. Some of them are over thirty-six years old! One day, as I sat and reminisced, I realized that my life story could be told through these writings. There were love letters from my husband, good wishes for our marriage, congratulations from family and friends, cards celebrating the births of our children, encouraging notes with scripture during the difficult times, condolences over the loss of parents and, more recently, get-well wishes after surgery.

I recalled an e-mail from a son when he was in Haiti and unable to join in a family gathering for the birthday of his dad, brother, and nephew. How special it was to me! I tried to figure out why it had touched me so much, and I decided that it was because I could read it over and over and digest all the thought and effort he had put into his message. He had thought about each person and customized the greetings to them.

Then I was reminded of the holy scriptures, God's love letters to us, and the way He used this method of letter writing to share His life story of love and redemption throughout generations. It was a story that had changed my life and the lives of multitudes. Letters written over two thousand years ago are still being used to change lives.

Thank You, Lord, for the letters that You wrote to us so that we could learn Your story of love and redemption, the letters that you used to change the story line of my life. Thank You for the hope we have of You continuing to work in the lives of others.

#SoupforSoul

> Then little children were brought to Jesus for him to place his hands on them and pray for them. But the disciples rebuked those who brought them. Jesus said. "Let the little children come to me, and do not hinder them, for the kingdom of heaven belongs to such as these." When he had placed his hands on them, he went on from there.
>
> —Matthew 19:13–15 (NIV)

It was Tuesday, my day for helping out at a local church where people could come for a meal. There were those who might not eat at all that day if it weren't for this ministry.

I enjoyed getting to know the people; many of the same faces showed up week after week. I looked forward to the camaraderie of working with others who also wanted to help, in hopes of meeting not only the physical needs but also the emotional and spiritual needs of others.

It was an ordinary day—but I'm always taken back when our ordinary days turn into something quite extraordinary, and I was surprised when I realized how God was using these people to minister to me.

As we finished the cleanup, there were a couple of new young moms whom I hadn't met before. I introduced myself to them and was getting to know them by asking them their children's ages and their names. They had two cousins in a double stroller, and when I doted over them, the biggest grins broke out on their cherubic faces. Two toddlers who were playing close by saw me, and when I said hi to the one little boy, he lifted up his arms to me. I lifted him up, and we exchanged hugs. The toddler girl stood at my feet, waiting for her turn, and then she, too, let me pick her up and hug her. I held on until they were ready to let go. I was so surprised that I found myself welling up in tears. I was trying to process my emotions. I know that I was missing my own children and wishing for some of their hugs, but it was more than that. I felt as if God were ministering to me through these little ones of His!

That year I had been on an emotional roller coaster. I had lost my dad and my father-in-law, had planned a wedding and, after raising four children, had an official empty nest. As if that weren't enough, I was in the beginning stages of menopause. While I looked forward to being alone again with my husband and searching for God's will for me in this new stage of life, something that had been such a big part of my life was now gone. My job as a mom was for the most part finished. I'd had very affectionate children, and I hadn't realized how much I missed their embraces.

It felt as though God were personally giving me hugs through these little children of His. Isn't it amazing that God knows our needs before we do?

Maybe that's why Jesus said to let the children come to Him. Maybe he was discouraged by the business of the world that He was ministering to and knew that His spirit would be lifted by those little ones, so He could go on with what He had been called to do.

Lord, I am always amazed at how You know our every need even before we know it. Thank You for using two of Your little ones today to encourage me.

#TangledMess

> Therefore, since we are surrounded by such a great cloud of witnesses, let us throw off everything that hinders and the sin that so entangles, and let us run with perseverance the race marked for us.
>
> —Hebrews 12:1 (NIV)

The first day of school had arrived. It had been a good summer, but I was looking forward to this first day, when I could give the house a good cleaning and organize in absolute solitude.

I ran nonstop around the house, throwing clothes in the washer and dryer, dusting, vacuuming, and organizing, not even taking time out for lunch. I made just one short phone call the entire day. I found myself frustrated that I still had uncompleted jobs even after having had the entire day to work uninterrupted.

That evening, I ran the children to the store to get the necessary school supplies, grabbed a bite to eat, and headed home. My daughter went to pull the clothes from the dryer to fold them, so she could dry some of her clothes. That's when she discovered a wad of laundry tangled in fishing line. Apparently, in my haste, I had scooped up a part of the line from a spool that was on the floor next to the dryer.

It had created a tangled web of wrinkled destruction. I picked up the pile, grabbed some scissors, and started cutting my way out of the tangle of line.

After I expressed how I wished the boys would keep their fishing line where it belonged, my daughter and the rest of the kids chuckled as they watched me work at untangling it. Seeing that I was tired from a long day and failing to appreciate the humor, my daughter decided to help lighten the moment. She said, "It's a lot like life, isn't it, Mom?" I thought about what she'd said as I continued to work at the puzzle of line.

As I continued trying to straighten out the mess, I thought of how the decisions we make entangle our lives. A bad decision can make our lives complicated and messy. A good decision can simplify life. I thought of our current president, whose term was "entangled" for a bad decision that was forcing me to talk to my children about things that are uncomfortable to talk about. I reflected on two marriages that I had learned in the last couple of weeks were about to dissolve because of poor decisions. I considered my daughter's discouragement that so many of her high school friends had made the decision to become sexually active and now their lives were being woven into a tangled mess because of it. I thought about how my daughter's friend's decisions were affecting her and their group of friends.

The one phone call I'd made that day had been to a single friend of mine who had both of her children starting new schools. I had called to see how her "mommy heart," as she called it, was doing. We'd talked about how hard it is letting go, and I told her how irritated I was that I couldn't get more done. She expressed frustration that she was so far behind that it looked like there was no catching up, but she told me she had decided to major on the majors and minor on the minors. A clean house is nice, and it helps our daily lives be more organized, but it isn't a major item in the scheme of life, and I need to remind myself of that while we have little people living with us.

Yes, we need to teach our children organizational skills and expect them to help around the house, but no, it isn't going to look like a furniture showroom. Man, I would love that, but it just isn't reality. If it did look like a showroom, no one would be comfortable living there, except for me. But I'm afraid I would be sitting in the "grouping" all alone—and I wouldn't want that.

Lord, thank You for the reminder of what's important right now and what isn't. I know I am in the busy stage of parenting, but I also know that I have these children you have loaned me for such a small window of time, and I don't want to miss what's really important. I need wisdom to know how to navigate through these uncharted waters, especially in a culture that is telling our children that right and wrong are relative. Help me to help them see that You, God, are the farthest thing from a killjoy but that You—out of your great love for us, the greatest love they will ever know—have given us guidelines for our protection and that only in a relationship with You will they discover genuine joy!

#UndertheWeather

> When evening came, many who were demon-possessed were brought to him, and he drove out the spirits with a word and healed all the sick. This was to fulfill what was spoken through the prophet Isaiah: "He took up our infirmities and carried our diseases."
>
> —Matthew 8 14–17 (NIV)

It is less than a week before Christmas. Mrs. Claus isn't getting much sleep, and it isn't because this momma wasn't trying to settle in for "a long winter's nap." It's because of a nasty head cold that started out with a sore throat and after three days turned into a full-fledged time-to-call-the-doctor bacterial infection.

I don't ever remember having such horrible nights with a cold. I did all the preparations to help me have a good night's rest. I had my water bottle close by for my dry throat, I had my Christmas decorator box of tissues by my bedside, and before I climbed into bed I took my antibiotic and prescription cough syrup. What could possibly go wrong? It had to be the reclining position, because no sooner had I laid down than it all started. The nose would stuff up, and then the cough would follow, and then my throat became so raw that I cringed when swallowing became necessary. I tried elevating my head, and when I couldn't tolerate the pain, I got up to gargle with salt water. Then I grabbed some throat lozenges and lay back down, and the cycle repeated itself all night long. Around five thirty in the morning I decided to try sitting up in a chair, and when I didn't have much success at getting any sleep, I drew a hot bath to help me relax and to produce some steam.

I was really starting to feel sorry for myself when I remembered my daughter's friend, who was then on a leave of absence. She was spending time with her mom who, after being diagnosed just a short time ago with Lou Gehrig's disease, was expected to live less than sixty days. I decided to turn my insomnia into a prayer time for this mom, who was experiencing firsthand the frailties of her body. Yes, there are many diseases and illnesses that can be cured, but there are still some that just ravage our bodies and render us powerless to change the outcome when our physical bodies wear out. There will always be suffering on this earth, but one day we will be freed from suffering for good because of the Christmas story, which is so much more than a story. It is a historical fact that a baby boy was born in a lowly stable in Bethlehem about two thousand years ago, and He changed not only the course of history but also the hearts of men and women. This continues to today, as He was born to die so that we could be reconciled to God.

God's people were waiting for Him to produce a king, but

this king just wasn't recognized when he came in the form of an infant—an infant who grew and taught truth like no one else could, because he *was* truth. He was put to death because he claimed to be God, claimed to have the ability to forgive sins, and—in spite of all his miracles and His explanation that He was the way, the truth and the life—there were still those who didn't believe that he was the Christ, "the anointed one." Nothing has changed. There are still those who speak of Jesus as a good man, a teacher, and a prophet but won't acknowledge that He was God in the flesh. There are still people who miss what He tried to convey. John 14:11 says, "Believe me when I say that I am in the Father and the Father is in me; or at least believe on the evidence of the miracles themselves."

As the week went on, my daughter called, saying she was getting sick. Our son, who was traveling with his three children, called to say he had the flu while he was driving. Upon their arrival, two of his children were also starting flu-like symptoms.

I also discovered that a friend in my ladies' Bible study group, who had been battling cancer, had learned that it had spread. Another friend had fallen and broken her shoulder. And every year at this time I couldn't help but think of some family friends who'd lost their son in a car accident and buried him on Christmas Eve.

It's never a good time to lose a loved one, but maybe we need to remember what the holiday season is really about—the birth of our Savior, rather than a day to make sure we get exactly what we want under that Christmas tree. Maybe thinking about God's perfect gift of Himself and a life everlasting when we leave this earth will ease our pain.

His life, which began as an infant, ended on a cross, and after three days—unlike my worsening cold—was resurrected!

Lord, thanks for the reminder that these frail bodies of ours will one day no longer be needed. Our earthly skin will be left behind and replaced by the new heavenly bodies that we will inherit when we enter into Your presence! As we wait, comfort those of us who are missing our loved ones and those who are suffering with imperfect earthly bodies. Help us to be uncomfortable with this skin that we live in now, knowing that You have so much more planned for us than what we can see here.

#WinSomeLoseSome

> My purpose is that they may be encouraged in heart and united in love, so that they may have the full riches of complete understanding, in order that they may know the mystery of God, namely, Christ, in whom are hidden all the treasures of wisdom and knowledge.

—Colossians 2:2 (NIV)

My eighty-two-year old mother passed on to me her appreciation of antiques as she dabbled in collecting in our home state of Indiana. So when I heard that there was going to be a road show of sorts, I thought she would enjoy taking some of her finds, to discover their value.

She had some Notre Dame memorabilia, some bronze bookends of Knute Rockne, and a pioneer coverlet that she'd bought at a secondhand store; it came with a note written by a mother to her son: "Merry Christmas 1984. This coverlet is called 'linsey-woolsey.' It was home woven 100 or more years ago (1855) back in Indiana by your great-great grandmother. They sheared the sheep, carded the wool, spun and wove it. Also, raised the flax to make the linen thread. We are sending you some of their heirlooms this year. Love, Mom and Dad." She also had some gold rings, a garnet, and a cameo. We were excited about going, and we made plans to get there early to avoid what we thought would be long lines.

My husband and I took a pocket watch that had been his father's, an old piece of sheet music, some antique dolls, and a plate that had come from my grandfather's mother.

At the road show, our number was finally called, and we carried in our treasures in anticipation of having them valued. We were actually approached by another seller who was interested in some GI Joe toys that I had brought. He had made me a verbal offer and was now offering to trade some vintage baseball cards. My husband was trying to talk me into making the trade, but I was sentimentally attached. I had bought them as an investment when my eldest son enlisted in the Marine Corps, and I decided I'd rather hold onto them for a few more years to see if it would increase in monetary value.

The lady doing the evaluating was very nice and took down our items one by one, giving us the scoop on each item. "Yes, this doll was one of the better brands from the 1940s, but in this slow economy, it's not a big call. A porcelain doll from this same company would bring a higher price." The blanket was beautiful, she informed us, but would need to be authenticated. It could bring several hundred dollars if it was the real thing. The garnet really didn't have much value, but the gold was worth something in both of the rings. The bookends were maybe worth forty dollars. The hundred-year-old copper kettle was nice, she told us, but it had been repaired, which lessened its value. My mom looked at me and said, "Well, win some, lose some."

We walked out a bit deflated upon realizing that we were carrying everything we had brought, with the exception of some pre-1964 silver coins. They wrote us a check for ninety dollars. Ninety dollars! All these "treasures" we'd been carrying around and moving from place to place over the last thirty-six years of marriage amounted to less than a hundred dollars!

It is fun to collect old things, but this verse kept coming to mind: "Do not store up for yourselves treasures on earth, where moth and rust destroy, and where thieves break in and steal. But store up for yourselves treasures in heaven, where moth and rust do not destroy, and where thieves do not break in and steal. For where your treasure is, there your heart will be also (Matthew: 6:19–21).

Lord, thank You for the reminder today that our "stuff" is nothing more than stuff. We expend a lot of time, energy, and money to buy stuff, keep our stuff, clean, and even store stuff when we get too much stuff. Help me to focus on spending my time, energies, and money on things that will speak to Your heart and will make a difference in eternity.

CHAPTER 7

GOD'S AMAZING CREATION

#AmazingLove

Are not two sparrows sold for a penny? Yet not one
of them will fall to the ground apart from the will
of your Father. And even the very hairs of your head
are all numbered. So, don't be afraid; you are worth
more than many sparrows.

—Matthew 10:31 (NIV)

I am learning to recognize those special gifts of reprieve from
routine that God sends our way; I am able to bask in the delight of
the moment and listen for His voice speaking to us through it.

Just the other day He brought one literally to my front door. As
I climbed the steps to my front door, I heard a squeaking sound.
I immediately thought *rodent*. My exterminator, Ralph, had just
told me that the perimeter of the house should be treated for these
creatures.

I peered into the underbrush, and sure enough, a rodent-like
head peered back at me. Trying to identify its classification, I
recognized it as a baby squirrel. When my son arrived home from
school and I told him about it, we agreed we would figure out a way
to protect it from the neighborhood dogs and cats and then try to
get it back to its mom.

I warned my son of the danger of rabies, so he found a towel and picked it up. We sat in the driveway, cuddling this little creature and pondering what its needs were. We found an eyedropper and fed it some milk. Soon the little guy started dozing, and my son made a warm nest for him in a bucket that we placed on the porch until morning.

As my son was leaving for school the next morning, he informed me that the mother was up in the tree above where we had found her baby. I told him to go ahead to the bus stop, and I would place the baby under the tree. I did that, and then I sat on the stoop and watched.

What I observed brought such joy and wonder as I thought of the incredible system our God has set up for the animal kingdom as well as for us. The mother watched a few minutes to be sure that there was no danger, and then she scurried down that tree and checked out the squeaking. She sniffed her baby, grabbed him by the midsection, and ran up that tree to redeposit him in the nest.

I thought of my children, all four of them in different stages of life, and was reminded that my Heavenly Father, the Creator of heaven and earth, loves them even more than I and is perfectly capable of protecting them when I can't be present.

This squirrel mom had come home to an empty nest, unaware of what her baby had experienced during its absence from her. The potential of danger for this little creature was great. Cars, cats, dogs, lawnmowers, people, or other rodents were all threats to her baby. Unbeknownst to the mother, her babies had been cared for and protected in her absence.

Thanks, Lord, for reminding me of how You care for me and my children, no matter where they are and what they are doing. Thanks for the pain of parenting—did I actually say that? Yes, thanks for the pain we go through, so I am able to fully appreciate how You have worked and are working in my life and the lives of my children. Thanks for walking with me and bringing me to this point where I can thank You.

#BadAdvice

I am the Real Vine and my Father is the Farmer. He cuts off every branch of me that doesn't bear grapes. And every branch that is grape-bearing he "prunes" back so it will bear even more. You are already pruned back by the message I have spoken. Live in me. Make your home in me just as I do in you. In the same way that a branch can't bear grapes by itself but only be being joined to the vine, you can't bear fruit unless you are joined with me.

—John 15: 1–4 (MSG)

We live in South Florida, and one of my favorite times of year is when the fruit trees blossom and the air is filled with the aroma of the blooms!

When we moved into our most recent home, our neighbors quickly pointed out to us a particular tangerine tree that was reputed to have an abundance of fruit with excellent flavor and a Key lime tree. Neighbors on both sides insisted that the reason they were so laden with fruit was because the trees were given an annual "beating." They proceeded to tell us we should get a rake out at least once a year, at a particular time, to beat the tree, and to be sure to scar the bark—we would reap the benefits!

Questioning the wisdom in this advice, the next time a county inspector came by to check our trees for disease, I asked his opinion about this theory. He explained that while beating the tree would put the tree into shock and thus cause it to produce more fruit, it would also open the tree up for other problems. When the bark was scarred, it would make the tree more susceptible to infestation by parasites and diseases. He then went on to explain that pruning the tree would produce the same result.

My husband, who is a landscape architect, explained that in the process of pruning a tree you carefully select particular branches to cut off, ones that bear no fruit, and trim clean those that do bear fruit so they will produce even more.

Isn't this the way we find ourselves thinking about life? Let's pull ourselves up by our bootstraps, take the bull by the horns, and do what we have to do to accomplish what we want to accomplish. We don't care who we might have to step on to get our way or what obstacles will come along. We will do what we have to do to come out on top!

The first and true gardener, God the Father, has a much better way. Jesus described himself as the true vine and His Father as the gardener. He cuts off every branch in us that bears no fruit, while every branch that does bear fruit he trims clean so that it will be even more fruitful. No branch can bear fruit by itself; it must remain on the vine. Neither can we bear fruit unless we remain in Him.

Lord, I'm so grateful that during the pruning seasons of my life You didn't beat me but carefully pruned me as a loving Father does, desiring only the best for me. Thank You for Your loving discipline rather than harsh punishment.

#Birdwatching

How many are your works, O Lord! In wisdom you made them all; the earth is full of your creatures.

—Psalm 104:24 (NLT)

It had taken a few years to fix up our backyard and turn it into an environment that birds would be attracted to. We'd allowed a few years of growth for the trees that we'd planted and time for the foliage to grow. It was now time to put up some birdhouses.

Because we had an abundance of wandering cats in our neighborhood, the environment had not been conducive to attracting birds to our yard. But between a fence and some electric wiring, our yard was now becoming a sanctuary for the birds and other creatures to enjoy.

My husband strategically hung up the feeders outside of the back family room where we ate the majority of our meals, so we could watch. We were having breakfast one morning, and sure enough, the most beautiful little bird landed on the feeder to gather some seed. He had the most beautiful orange-colored chest and indigo head and a bright-green mark on his back. We quickly got out the bird identification book and discovered he was a painted bunting. With the screens off the window and the camera ready, we enjoyed getting some great shots of this beautiful creature.

This bird now comes by almost daily, and it has become part of our routine, one that my husband and I are quite thrilled with. The children are gone, the house is quieter, and we are getting to know each other again without distractions. We are finding that what attracted us to each other in the first place, some forty years ago, is still there! We remember enjoying spending time just being together, and while that hasn't changed, we are discovering that with the extended time we have together, we still share many of the same interests—and one of them is bird watching!

Lord, thank You for this new, quieter stage of life with my groom. It is different—it is definitely quieter—but it is good, and we are learning to slow down a bit and enjoy what You have for us in this new season of life.

#FavFlower

"Come now, let us argue this out," says the Lord. "No matter how deep the stain of your sins, I can remove it. I can make you as clean as freshly fallen snow. Even if you are stained as red as crimson, I can make you as white as wool."

—Isaiah 1:18 (NLT)

I took my cup of coffee outside one morning, to breathe in the fresh spring air and to glimpse the little flower garden that I was trying to get started. In the middle of my garden is a gardenia tree that my husband planted for me. The gardenia blooms in the spring; it produces a most vivid white flower with the most wonderful, indescribable fragrance.

The blooms are gone, though, as quickly as they come. They wither within a day or two, and the lily-white petals lose their fragrance and turn into limp, tea-stained clumps of dried-up petals. This process happens so quickly that it is hard to believe that these sodden lumps were so beautiful just a day or so earlier. When the flowers turn, new buds break forth, so you enjoy daily the beauty of the new blooms and the decay of those whose life is over. It is truly a cycle-of-life tree.

I removed the dead blooms so that when I looked at the tree all I could see was the brilliance of the white against the background of the dark-green leaves. The dead flowers were ruining the beauty of the new blooms. I couldn't fully appreciate their beauty without removing the "has-beens."

The whiteness of the gardenia flower is the purest form of white. I don't even think any of the paint companies have captured this shade of brilliance. I was reminded of our lives as I thought of how some days we can be beautiful to others and then there are those days when we are ugly and no one wants to be around us. I was also reminded that the only way we can be beautiful to people is to have the stain of our sins removed. If we will only trust God, and obey Him, and let Him help, He tells us, He will make us as clean as freshly fallen snow. I was also reminded that when God is in our lives, He doesn't see the decay in us at all but only His radiance, covering our ugliness.

What God has done for us is what many try to do with cosmetics or surgery. Have you ever had a friend who has shared with you what they believe is a physical "flaw" in them? I have friends who have pointed out their "flaws," but when I look at them I don't see flaws at all. In fact, what they consider flaws might be what I believe makes them unique. Before I put on my makeup, I see myself as I am, not how I want the world to see me. In fact, I will go to great detail and great expense to cover up those "flaws" that I see. When I walk out of my home into the world, they see something quite different, something better than my bare face.

We all want to be accepted and, most of all, loved. Just as friends love us no matter what we look like, God also loves us with the purest form of love.

Lord, please remove the ugly, dingy things in my life, and each day work in me so that when others look at me they don't see me at all but You, a light so pure, so beautiful, and whiter than a gardenia petal. And Lord, when I get the opportunity, I'll tell them that the same being who created the gardenia shrub is who they see—not me but You in me. I will tell them that I had heart surgery performed on me by the Great Physician, as no cosmetic surgeon has been or ever will be capable of. And it was free!

#IfTreesCouldTalk

A man cannot be established through wickedness,
but the righteous cannot be uprooted.

—Proverbs 12:3 (NIV)

As my husband and I were eating our breakfast at the same table that we did most mornings, I found myself staring out the window at the majestic pine tree across our canal, on the other side of the next street. It is perfectly framed by the window in our Florida room, and I asked my husband what there was about that tree that caused me to stare at it so much.

He answered that he often stared at it as well, and as we continued eating our oatmeal, he pointed out that it was the highest tree around. "Because it is, the sun reaches it first, so we can enjoy the glow that comes in the mornings and evenings. Because of its size, I would guess that it was probably planted about the time we were born." He continued, "It has weathered a lot of storms throughout the years." This conversation ensued during a particular sad time in the life of one of our children, and as the two of us sat there sharing why we thought this tree obviously meant something to both of us, we simultaneously started to cry and then laugh all at the same time. We then talked about how much it had survived, and we felt a newfound respect for it.

We continued. I asked, amongst my sobs, "Why do you think it survived when so many trees didn't?" He said that pine trees are difficult to relocate because of their tap roots. "Their roots are so big and go so deep into the ground that they can withstand strong winds." And I knew I had my answer: The righteous cannot be uprooted.

We are righteous not by what we do or do not do; we are righteous because we've been drawn to God and accepted His offer for the forgiveness of our sins. We are therefore declared righteous because of the forgiveness we have received through the work of Christ. Why will we survive this latest storm? Because our roots are deep, like those of that tree. The tree needs heavy roots to sustain it during storms, and so do we.

Thank You, Lord, for giving us this picture today of Your great love for us and for drawing us closer not only to You but to each other. Thank You for the encouragement that being rooted in You will assure us survival, whatever storms come our way. When the storms are over, we will be standing just as majestically as that tree.

#LousyShepherd

For this is what the Sovereign Lord says: I myself
will search for my sheep and look after them. As
a shepherd looks after his scattered flock when he
is with them, so will I look after my sheep. I will
rescue them from all the places where they were
scattered on a day of clouds and darkness.

—Ezekiel 34:11 (NIV)

On a tour to Alaska once, we were in an area where Dall sheep,
the ones with the distinctive curly horns, are known to make their
home atop craggy mountaintops.

As our guide spotted some, he told us to first point out the white
spots with our naked eyes along the top of the mountain and then
to focus in on that spot with our binoculars. As hard as I tried, and
with several different people desperately trying to point out the exact
location, describing particular peaks and ravines in an effort to help
me, I just couldn't find them. I was getting frustrated and reluctantly
came to the conclusion that I was obviously sheep-spotting disabled!

The more I thought about it, the more life application this
moment was bringing. Scripture came to mind. Disabled I am. "We
all, like sheep, have gone astray, each of us has turned to his own
way; and the Lord has laid on him the iniquity of us all" (Isaiah
53:6 NIV). "I am the good shepherd; I know my sheep and my
sheep know me just as the Father knows me and I know the Father
and I lay down my life for the sheep. I have other sheep that are not
of this sheep pen. I must bring them also. They too will listen to
my voice, and there shall be one flock and one shepherd" (John 10:
14–16 NIV).

I sure couldn't locate these sheep, unlike my good shepherd, who
not only recognizes each of his sheep but knows the exact spot to
find each and every one of them. He knows them by name and He

guides them to protect them from dangerous situations. "My sheep listen to my voice; I know them, and they follow me. I give them eternal life, and they shall never perish; no one can snatch them out of my hand. My Father, who has given them to me, is greater than all, no one can snatch them out of my Father's hand. I and the Father are one" (John 10: 27).

The next day my husband, the consummate wildlife observer—ornithology was one of favorite college courses, need I say more?—stopped along another site where Dall sheep had been spotted. I wasn't even going to try this time; I chose to stay in the car, along with some friends who had also seen enough of this species of sheep. I sat and watched him as he keenly and patiently scanned the tops of the mountains in hopes of discovering the whereabouts of the sheep. I just couldn't get over not only how interested he was in looking at them but the way he tirelessly kept up the search, as if he had some personal stake in locating them. Again I was reminded of the story Jesus told about the shepherd who lost one sheep and left the other ninety-nine to search for the one until he found it. Man, I know that wouldn't be the job for me. I'm afraid that the sheep would be out of luck, as I would give up the hunt after only a few minutes! But our Good Shepherd, thankfully, isn't like me. Just as we are happy when we find something we have lost, Jesus says, "I tell you that in the same way there will be more rejoicing in heaven over one sinner who repents than over ninety-nine righteous persons who do not need to repent."

Lord, thank You for making my husband so different from me and for being the good shepherd who knows me by my name, knows everything about me, and still loves me in the greatest way there is to demonstrate love to someone, by giving Your life for me. "Love each other as I have loved you. Greater love has no one than this that he lay down his life for his friends" (John 15:12–13). One of your thankful sheep friends.

#LoveIsintheAir

With persuasive words she led him astray; she seduced him with her smooth talk. All at once he followed her like an ox going to the slaughter, like a deer stepping into a noose till an arrow pierces his liver, like a bird darting into a snare, little knowing it will cost him his life.

–Proverbs 7:21–23 (NLT)

The men in my family go a little crazy when spring brings open season on wild turkeys. This is the official turkey courtship season, which has the species in the mood for love!

I have heard my husband talking about wild turkey hunting for years, have watched him go turkey hunting for all that time, and have even gone a couple of times with him. I'm still trying to figure out the allure. He has done lots of different kinds of hunting, but while he will skip other hunts, when turkey season comes a-calling, he's got his camo close by. I know he has passed on his love of the woods to his boys in a way that I wish I had been able to pass on my passions—I think the turkey won out!

As I was writing today, I had two calls from kids—telephone calls, that is—and there was turkey talk in all the conversations. My son who had just gotten off a tugboat for the first time in five months went up to Georgia with a friend and was stoked because early that morning, they bagged their first bird of the season. I really think he took time off just because of turkey season; in fact, I'm sure of it! He then talked about his other brother finally getting one. Apparently it isn't that easy. My third son called and said that he was disappointed because by the time we came to see him in May the turkey season would be over.

After hunting with my husband, I know that the turkeys are known for showing off for the opposite sex, strutting their stuff.

Maybe men get their sexual prowess from these birds? It involves the hunter taking on the role of the female, calling to the male turkey to lure him in to his demise.

I recently read a book that was gifted to my husband by a good friend. It was called "A Look at Life from a Deer Stand," by Steve Chapman. I eagerly read it, looking for some insight into my main squeeze and my sons. For wives of hunters, it has some good ideas why your man and your boys love it so much in the woods. It's a highly recommended read!

If you happen to be married to a turkey hunter or have boys who are into hunting, you best let them go once in a while, because the passion runs deep. You may consider a trip into the woods to experience, as my husband explains, the "thrill of turkeys calling back and cautiously moving to you as they begin to strut and gobble back." When I asked my husband to explain in more detail, he said, "I guess that it is the thrill to see how God has created His creatures to live out the way they were designed to desire their mate, to see the cycle of life in action." I still don't quite understand the allure of turkey hunting, but I have finally acquiesced to the fact that if I let him satisfy that desire to turkey hunt, there is a good possibility I will reap the benefits of a satisfied mate for the rest of the year!

If you are married to one of my sons (or will be) maybe if you let him get out during turkey season he will make a better mate the rest of the year!

When the boys were young, I struggled with trying to get them to buckle down for homework, but when it came to turkey calls, they would practice for hours. Maybe they get frustrated with us as women and decide they have a better chance out in the field?

I'm learning that God uses his animal kingdom to teach spiritual lessons to men and boys. My husband has told our boys, "Don't be stupid like a turkey!" By that he means to be lured to his demise by the "smooth talk" of a woman. That is a word picture from their dad that I, as their mom, would be incapable of teaching.

Dear Lord, thank You for the way you created us, male and

female. As men and women, we sometimes find our differences difficult to understand, but the older I get the more I see that You knew exactly what You were doing in every detail. It is me who has the limited vision. Thank You for revealing new things to me daily about Your incredibly complex Creation, including the male species!

#NervousNellie

You will keep in perfect peace those whose minds are steadfast, because they trust in you.

—Isaiah 26:3 (NIV)

I had just pulled out of my driveway and was headed toward the main traffic light, where I would make a left-hand turn out of my neighborhood, when I saw a little female anole on the hood of my car who appeared to be in great distress! She wasn't wasting any time in trying to find some immediate cover from the gale-force winds that she was encountering. She (I say *she* because of her size) was scurrying around in an effort to find a place of refuge for her itty-bitty lizard body. Just a few short minutes ago her life as a little lizard had been going quite well on the warm hood of my car in my driveway, but now the world as she had known it had been turned upside down.

I took glances at her as I tried to pay attention to traffic at the same time, and she made a dash for the wipers for some protection. Not feeling out of danger yet, she darted across to the antenna and really got whipped around as my speed increased. I felt bad, but I was reminded of my dad's admonition not to cause an accident for fear of killing an animal. "It would be better to kill a dog or cat than put a human at risk." She had her little legs wrapped around that wire and was holding on for her dear lizard life! When she saw that this effort wasn't working, she made quite a daring jump, taking me by surprise, back toward the wipers and down into the underbody of the hood, where I will never know whether her story had a happy ending or a sad one.

I found myself relating to the poor little gal, as I happened to be dealing this particular month with all kinds of changes in my own life that had me feeling quite outside my comfort zone. It started with switching my cable company to save eighty-five dollars a month. That meant changing my phone number, memorizing a new one after having had the old one for ten years and being handed a new remote that took me days to figure out, even with the help of my husband. I guess you could say I was feeling pretty tech savvy after mastering that, so when my phone died the next week and the salesman tried to upgrade me to a touch phone, I put all reasoning aside and said to myself, "You can do it!" I had just read an article about a guy who hated change. Believe me, I understood where he was coming from, but I had recently decided to fight my fear of change. I wasn't ready to cry uncle and join the many voices of my generation who were refusing to learn new technology.

I'm just not ready to admit I'm too old to be taught new tricks! I'm now an e-mailing, Facebooking, texting, online banking, picture-taking, and picture-forwarding techie! By the time this is printed, I'll probably already be out of touch with technology, but let me enjoy my moment of glory! LOL.

I can't believe it—I just got another call to tell me about another new way to save on my TV bill. "Pride comes before the fall." I am not changing it again! I hate change! I find that I'm allowing all of this technology stuff to consume me and make me a nervous wreck! What do we do in these stress-filled situations? Well, often we run around like crazed, scared-for-our-lives anoles, our heads bobbing in panic mode. It was good for me to watch the gal, albeit that I was looking into a mirror to see myself running around like a wiry, scared little amphibian.

If I'd thought the little anole would understand, I would have shared with her the verses that came to my mind: "Do not be anxious about anything, but in everything, by prayer and petition, with thanksgiving, present your request to God. And the peace of God, which transcends all understanding, will guard your hearts and your minds in Christ Jesus." Philippians 4: 6, 7 (NIV)

Lord, I desperately need that peace that can only be found in you.

#OnTask

And we know that in all things God works for the good of those who love him, who have been called according to his purpose.

—Romans 8:28 (NLT)

I was finally getting out of the house for a much needed walk after a long, cold winter; one of the coldest winters I have personally experienced in South Florida since moving here in 1977.

The refreshing 60 degrees actually seemed warm after the much colder temperatures. As I rounded the corner from my house, I spotted a woodpecker diligently doing what woodpeckers do, pecking his way through a telephone pole. I paused to watch, intrigued by the intensity with which he was working.

As I continued my walk, I saw another pole that had recently been replaced by our local utility company because of damage by woodpeckers. There had been so many holes bored into the old one that the company had had to remove it. The new pole had a greater diameter and a sleeve of metal wire to protect it from these birds!

All I could think about was my own life and how I wished it was that clear to me what my mission was each day. When the woodpeckers wake up, they clearly know what their mission is, and they get right to it. I know that part of my dilemma is that my role in life as a mom was very clear for years. I, too, woke up and knew that my days would be filled with the duties of being a wife and mom, and I relished all that the calling entailed.

Once my last child left home, I found that there were definitely more hours in the day for me to use as I chose. This was quite a change, and while I was delighted to have some "me" time, I found it difficult to figure out just how to spend my time.

I had time now to take the quiet walks that had been just a dream before, time to leisurely read a book if that was my desire, maybe time to write that book that I had talked about for years. But at other times I would find the new quiet deafening, it was so foreign to me. I had always wanted to write about raising a family, but when the last child left, I felt as if I had lost all my good material! But a friend reminded me that I needed to write about this new stage of life, post children; she was currently struggling with that stage as well. It was now time to explore how I would like to spend my time and to ask God to help me discover and adjust to the new mission He had for me. In the new quiet I found that I was learning to hear that small, still voice, not yet an audible voice but an internal prompting that brought new desires and ideas for this new life as an empty nester. I also found out that my husband had ideas about how I could be of help to him, and of course, that was where I had started my life as a married woman, with a desire to be his helpmate. So here I was, come full circle back to where we'd started as a couple.

I don't have it sorted out yet, but I wake up each morning and ask God to reveal to me His desires for the day. He is showing me day by day, and I'm going to attempt to go about my tasks every bit as diligently as that woodpecker.

Lord, You have been with me through every season of life so far, and I know You will continue to walk with me through this next, quieter, season. Show me what You have for me, and help me to live each day with the same passion I had for motherhood!

#UglyStump

> Who has believed our message and to whom has
> the arm of the Lord been revealed? He grew up
> before him like a tender shoot, and like a root out
> of dry ground. He had no beauty or majesty to
> attract us to him, nothing in his appearance that
> we should desire him. He was despised and rejected
> by mankind, a man of suffering, and familiar with
> pain. Like one from whom people hid their faces he
> was despised, and we held him in low esteem.
>
> —Isaiah 53:1–3 (NIV)

Because of my husband's love of plants and trees, it isn't unusual for him to move them around our yard the way I move furniture around inside our house.

There is a side yard behind our fence where we have a small garden and where we hide our trash containers. I noticed a while ago that my husband had planted what looked like nothing more than a large stump in one of the recycling containers. I would have thrown away the unsightly thing, but I ignored it and kept to the inside of the house. I wondered why he had stuck that thing into the soil but never really got around to asking.

On a recent trip to the recycle bin, I was taken aback when I saw that where the ugly stump had been there was now a beautiful specimen of a bougainvillea tree, with gorgeous fuchsia-colored blooms! How could something so ugly have turned into such a thing of beauty?

I asked my husband whether he had seen what the stump had turned into. He explained to me that the tree's root system had been damaged, and because of that it would have died, so he'd stripped it of all its leaves, which would have taken water away from the root system, so it would have a chance to be healthy again! I asked him what else he had been doing to the plant, and he explained that he had put it in good soil and had been watering and fertilizing it.

Amazing! What parallels we find in God's plant world. The root system of a plant or tree is crucial to its health. Without it the tree will die. Scripture tells us that trusting in the Lord is like the root system of a tree, the thing that will keep us spiritually healthy, "serene and calm through droughts with no worries" (Jeremiah 17:8 MSG).

How do we make sure we have healthy root systems? It begins with trusting the Lord in spite of our circumstances. He, like the stump in my yard, was passed by unnoticed. How often do we get so absorbed in our own lives that we ignore the One who is the giver of life?

Lord, thank you for Your Creation and the way You have used it to reveal to us your deep spiritual truths. Just like this stump, You, the King of Kings, the Savior of the world, remained unnoticed. But is in and through you that my ugliness and the ugliness of all who trust in You is made beautiful in Your time. Abiding in You, our root system, is what makes us burst forth in beauty indescribable.

#YesterdayTodayandTomorrow

Keep your lives free from the love of money and be content with what you have, because God has said, "Never will I leave you; never will I forsake you." So we can say with confidence, "The Lord is my helper; I will not be afraid. What can man do to me?" Remember your leaders, who spoke the word of God to you. Consider the outcome of their way of life and imitate their faith. Jesus Christ is the same yesterday and today and forever.

—Hebrews 13:5–8 (NIV)

The yesterday-today-and-tomorrow plant is a tropical shrub with two beautiful shades of purple mixed with a pure white bloom. It has petals of deep violent, a medium lavender, and white. It is stunning to look at when in full bloom. All three colors are seen at the same time, because new blooms emerge each day during its blooming season.

A friend gave me this shrub as a gift years ago when I moved into a new home, saying that she had been my friend yesterday, was today, and would be tomorrow. What a nice gift and sentiment. Ironically, this friend and I no longer stay in touch.

I have a faithful friend, though, who has been there for me through thick and thin and has never let me down. Circumstances change, friendships wane, commitments are broken, dreams are shattered, and loved ones die—but through it all there is friend that will never disappoint you. He is unchanging. He was there for me yesterday, is here for me today, and will be with me forever! His love is constant and available to all.

Oh, and as for God's perfect design of the plant world, I just learned that the deep purple bloom lasts one day, fades to the lighter shade of violet on the second day, and on the third day turns white and then dies and drops off. What a picture of Christ. Yesterday is purple, the color of royalty, the long-awaited King. Today is lavender, and tomorrow is white, the righteousness we gain when we accept His work on the cross. And on the third day the bloom drops. Our Savior died, but unlike these petals, he arose on the third day.

Lord, I am always amazed at and still learning about how all of Your Creation points to You and what you did for us! Thank You for revealing Yourself in such incredible detail and beauty all around us!

CHAPTER 8

SEASONS OF CHANGE

#AllAboutMe

So come, let us worship: bow before him, on your
knees before God, who made us! Oh yes he's our God,
and we're the people he pastures, the flock he feeds.

—Psalm 95:6–7 (MSG)

I was doing some Christmas shopping in a favorite store of mine
when I came across a ceramic teapot with the words "Come Let Us
Adore Me" inscribed on it.

A couple of women noticed the same piece of pottery at the
same time I did. I purposely lingered, as I was curious what their
reaction would be. Their reaction was quite different than mine.
They started talking about how cute it was and how it would be a
perfect gift for some of their friends. I would guess these were high-
maintenance friends!

I was taken aback, as I have always associated the word *adore*
with the hymn I grew up singing every Christmas Eve, "Come Let
Us Adore Him." The lyrics resonated in my head:

Oh, come let us adore Him,
Oh, come let us adore Him,
Oh, come let us adore Him,
Christ the Lord.

For You alone are worthy,
For You alone are worthy,
For You alone are worthy,
Christ the Lord.

We'll give You all the glory,
We'll give You all the glory,
We'll give You all the glory,
Christ the Lord.

The lyrics will give you an idea why that inscription was disturbing me to the core. The words started running through my mind as I processed the words: *Let us adore Him; You alone are worthy; we'll give You all the glory.*

The reason I was out shopping was to look for gifts to give family and friends in celebration of the birth of Jesus Christ, the greatest gift mankind has ever received. He is the reason we participate in gift giving at this time of year.

I realize our culture has gotten far away from the real meaning of Christmas, but the inscription urging us to adore ourselves stopped me in my tracks. It was so blatant—just so telling of how far we have drifted from worshipping God to worshipping ourselves. Even though I recognize this tendency in our culture and myself, to see it in print seemed a mockery of our Creator.

Dear Lord, thank You for the reminder that, apart from You, our tendency is to adore ourselves. Lord, forgive all of us for being prone to wandering away from you and elevating ourselves above You, our Creator.

#BabyGrand

For you created my inmost being; you knit me together in my mother's womb. I praise you because

I am fearfully and wonderfully made; your works
are wonderful, I know that full well.

—Psalm 139:13–14 (NIV)

Olivia is our yet unborn granddaughter, who is due in December.
Though the world has not met her yet, she has everything, at eighteen
weeks in utero that she will physically need to survive on this earth.
Amazing! She just needs to gain some weight. If she is anything like
her grandmother, this will be a breeze!

My daughter just sent an ultrasound of her with a text message.
"The painting is coming along." She was referring to the room
that she and my son-in-law were readying to welcome Olivia, but
I thought about the work of the artist who was forming her in my
daughter's womb as we spoke. Yes, the painting is coming along!

It has been so much fun watching them get excited to meet their
daughter and welcome her into the world. My daughter said that her
husband asked her, "What will I do with her? Will she play catch
with me?" My daughter, a daughter herself, wisely assured him that
their daughter will enjoy doing anything that he wants to do, that
she will just enjoy being with him.

It took me back to our family vacations, which often revolved
around the water and fishing. Because we both loved these kind of
vacations, and because we had three boys, we probably did more
guy-type vacations in an effort to keep everyone entertained, but
I don't think she really minded. I remembered a particular family
video where we were at a Florida spring and were bathing the kids
at the end of a long day on the water. A little bit of fishing, a little
bit of snorkeling, a lot of swimming, and she was sitting in the
kiddie pool. At the stage where she was missing her two front teeth,
she said, "I've been fishing all my days. I'm hot, I'm tired, and I'm
irritable!" In another month we will vacation with our daughter and
son-in-law—yes, in the boat, at her suggestion. This time we will

hunt for scallops. It will be hot, August in Florida, and we will be tired and maybe irritable, but we will be together.

A father's love runs deep for a daughter, and likewise a daughter's love runs deep for her daddy. Olivia's daddy is already talking of ways he plans to protect her and is already announcing to a large audience that his daughter will be here soon. He has a business in which they do a lot of advertising, and he has announced that a girl is on the way! It is so endearing and a reminder of how special a father's love is. Today I am missing my earthly father who is no longer with us. But it also fun to see the cycle of life and to be reminded today that when I leave this earth I will be welcomed into my heavenly Father's arms, the arms of the One who formed me in my mother's womb. Whatever the work of my Father will be in eternity, I will just be so glad to be spending time with him!

Lord, I thank You for the gift of children and grandchildren. Thank you for the design of the family unit, and thank you for this precious baby who we are about to welcome into the family.

#BustingaGroove

He set off. When he got to the outskirts of Damascus, he was suddenly dazed by a blinding flash of light.

—Acts 9:3 (MSG)

After I had climbed into the comfort of my bed one night, a phone call came, and the voice of one of my three sons was on the other end. He was sharing with me the events of his shopping experience with his niece, my granddaughter, for her tenth birthday.

As he was busy establishing a new business, I had offered to give him one of the small gifts I had on hand, so he didn't have to worry about going shopping for a gift before we all took her out for lunch. But he'd said that he really wanted to take her shopping to pick out something she wanted. He was in a very talkative state, and as a mom I have learned to listen when those opportunities come, whether or not the timing is good for me. You can't schedule those quality moments, and moms live for those moments; this was a big part of the reason my husband and I decided I would be a stay-at-home mom.

I wasn't prepared for just how special this conversation was to be. This kid—young adult of twenty-four—was lit up as I had never seen him! What I heard coming out of his mouth was leaving me with a wide range of emotions, from exceeding joy that brought tears of happiness to unbelief at what I was hearing.

You see, this was the son who had been involved in the accident that had tragically ended in a fatality in the other vehicle. This accident had changed his life. I have yet to understand exactly how, even though we had talked about it at length. He had shared how, a couple of days after the accident, he had pulled his car over and found himself uncontrollably crying out to God. He'd told us that at that moment he'd asked God to take control of his life. "Mom, I heard this guy speak, and he was talking about living in this culture and how it is the exact opposite of how God intends for us to live." He was specifically talking about dating, and while he truly wanted to find a soul mate to do life with, he was frustrated with the process. I believe he was realizing that the way he had been dating was unhealthy.

The closest word I can use to describe his enthusiasm and conviction about the topic he was discussing is *electrifying*! I love to dance, and if I could, I'd love to be able to dance as John Travolta does in "Dance Fever." The exhilaration in this song could be compared to the level of passion that I was hearing in my son's voice as he skipped from topic to topic.

He then jumped to something I had said over lunch. "Mom. You know what you said, how you used to work at a newspaper and you really had a brain before you decided to become a mom? That is not true! Being a mom—being my mom—was important!"

I did think of how we'd tried to explain these things to him during his high school years, but I now understand that it just wasn't the time then for him to get it. There is a tendency to think, *Why did I waste my breath? Did they hear anything I said?* But then I remembered when I used to go to Youth for Christ "burger bashes." What I heard there made so much more sense than what I heard my parents saying. God just used other people besides my parents to bring me to an understanding of His Love.

All I could think was, *Okay, Lord, I can die now.* I know that sounds silly, but my son was exactly right in what he said about the culture we live in. It does not value motherhood—but he was telling me he did!

Now, if I could just encourage moms to not give up, to pray, and teach, and be there through all the tough stuff, and draw boundaries when necessary. Even though they may get discouraged, I am here to report that I have witnessed a changed life, an electrified life, and it is a sight to behold!

Lord, thank You for allowing me to live long enough to witness this change. Thank You for the earthly reminder that there will be yet another change and it, too, will be in a flash. I may not have gotten as much sleep as normal tonight, but I witnessed a changed life, and it was a flash, a glimpse into the future. Lord, encourage moms today who are in the trenches and can see no glimmer of hope. Help them to not grow weary, strengthen them, encourage them, and put others around them to hold them up until their precious children encounter You, the Light of the world.

#ClearerVision

Therefore we are always confident and know that
as long as we are at home in the body we are away

from the Lord. We live by faith, not by sight. We are
confident, I say, and would prefer to be away from
the body and at home with the Lord.

—Corinthians 5:6–8 (NIV)

Have you noticed that your spouse, friends, or family members
are starting to do things like tucking your shirt tag in, telling you
that your zipper needs zipping, or making you aware of hair growing
on your face or ears (where it never grew before)?

It took me some time to get to the keyboard this morning, as I
was on an intent search for my reading glasses, which have become
more necessary than I ever could have imagined. My inability to see
as clearly as I once did often feels like a nuisance, but I am coming to
understand that it can be quite the opposite. Maybe it's even part of
a greater plan by God, like so many things that we won't understand
until we are there. I was looking forward to a day of staying at home
to do some organization and a bit of decorating. I showered and was
putting my face on at my leisure, something I used to dream about
doing when my children were small. What you fail to realize when
you're a young mom is that by the time you get to this stage, you
will be surprised to see (or maybe not *see*) that this morning ritual
will change. It will include a ten-power magnification mirror, and
you will see things that you never thought could grow on your face!

In a shop, I had seen pine cones placed in a big round wooden
bowl, so I was taking pine cones that I had collected from outings
out of the basket that I had them in and moving them to an old
wooden bowl. When I reached into the bottom of the basket without
my glasses, I removed what I thought to be a twig. But I realized
upon picking it up that I was holding a petrified lizard.

You may ask, what is so great about this stage? As you are
changing, don't forget that your spouse is growing older as well. In
God's perfect timing, your sight starts dimming so that you see each
other as you remember each other.

"For we live by faith, not by sight" (2 Corinthians 5:7 NIV). As I grow older, Lord, I thank You for the reminder and the clearer vision that living by believing and not seeing was your plan all along. As I come closer to being taken to my real home with You, You have given me and my husband a visual of what You really meant by that verse. Strengthen my spiritual vision, Lord.

#FeelingFit

> A twinkle in the eye means joy in the heart, and good news makes you feel fit as a fiddle.
>
> —Proverbs 15:30 (MSG)

We all like to get a good health report when we go to the doctor, but as we age there is a very good chance that we will eventually have to hear some not-so-good news. We realize that our bodies are not designed to last forever, at least not in their physical stage. The deterioration process begins right after birth!

Everyone knows what you have to do to stay in good physical shape. Diet, exercise, plenty of sleep and avoidance of and or moderation of certain substances that have proven to either shorten your life span and or make your later years with a lesser quality of life.

As mentioned previously, I'd had symptoms of a tight chest and a cough at one time, and because of some heart disease in my family history, my doctor had ordered tests. I'd started checking Internet sites to see if I could diagnose myself. (Hmm, could be anxiety, but I'm not really an anxious person. Allergies? I've never had them, but they can develop as you age. Maybe the statin drug I'm on?) I went for a walk the morning I was going to hear the results of my tests. I started reading in Proverbs, a book written by King Solomon, who was known as the wisest man on earth. The book of Proverbs is considered a manual for living.

The subtitle was "Don't Assume You Know It All." I love the Message version of the Bible because it is one that is easy for me to understand. Wow, isn't that characteristic of our culture in this age of information at our fingertips? It got my attention! This is how God speaks to us, through His written word. I started to read, "Good friend, don't forget all I've taught you; take to heart my commands. They'll help you live a long, long time, a long life lived full and well." Wow! I would like to live a long life full and well, wouldn't you? It made me want to sit up and pay attention to His commands. I skipped down to verse 5: "Trust God from the bottom of your heart; don't try to figure out everything on your own. Listen for God's voice in everything you do, everywhere you go, and he's the one who will keep you on track. Don't assume that you know it all. Run to God! Run from evil! Your body will glow with health, your very bones will vibrate with life!" Wouldn't I like to have that kind of glow! You can bet that's a glow that no chemist has been able to bottle. Strong bones? I thought milk would do the body good!

Then we are cautioned to "never walk away." "Dear friend, guard Clear thinking and common Sense with your life; don't for a minute lose sight of them. They'll keep your soul alive and well, they'll keep you fit and attractive. You'll travel safely, you'll neither tire not trip, you'll take afternoon naps without a worry, and you'll enjoy a good night's sleep" (Proverbs 3:21–24 (MSG). Sounds like some great medical benefits don't you agree?

But that is where the monumental difference lies: knowledge versus wisdom. We can either have lots of knowledge and no wisdom, or not be very knowledgeable and have lots of wisdom. If I had to choose for myself or for my children, I would choose wisdom. Knowledge is information, which is what our culture has much of, but we are sorely lacking in the area of wisdom.

Lord, I thank You for leaving us Your word. Your words of truth often contradict what we hear out in the world. I thank You that you didn't leave us alone without any instructions for how to survive and to thrive in this world until you take us to our real home to spend eternity with you! Your good news has me feeling as fit as a fiddle!

#FloweringWeed

> For the kind of sorrow God wants us to experience
> leads us away from sin and results in salvation. There's
> no regret for that kind of sorrow. But worldly sorrow,
> which lacks repentance, results in spiritual death.
>
> —2 Corinthians 7:10 (NLT)

Our two youngest boys were off for the week of spring break, the week prior to Easter. They had been looking forward to fishing the entire week. With each new day, they would rise early and come home after they'd caught what there was to catch, or earlier if the seas were too rough.

Upon hearing the return of their boat, I would walk down the steps to the dock to view their catch. During my treks up and down that week, I had noticed a weed that was wedged between the steps and small hedge alongside. It looked as if it were going to flower, so I left it there and observed its transformation throughout the week.

As the week progressed, the flower bloomed into the most beautiful sunflower-like blossom. Thinking about Easter, I was reminded of the resurrection and my new life in Christ.

Toward the end of the week, when the boat arrived home once again, the boys proudly displayed a big tuna that they had caught. As I sat on the steps watching them cut it into steaks, the phone rang. It was our daughter, who was working through a difficult time in her life. The little flowering weed began to take on more and more meaning, and I thought of how our lives might get weedy but how God takes those weedy situations and weedy choices we make and turns them (and us) into beautiful flowers.

Thank You, Lord, for the power of the resurrection. Thank You for transforming us from pesky weeds into beautiful flowers.

#HaironFleek

The glory of the young is their strength; the gray hair of experience is the splendor of the old.

—Proverbs 20:29 (NIV)

A good friend of mine who is a hairstylist was in my area and stopped by to see me recently. She was having a "harried" day (no pun intended!), so we went to a little café to get a cup of cappuccino to relax a few minutes and to catch up on each other's lives.

As we sat down, she looked at me or, more accurately, looked at my roots and said, "You need to have your roots done! Look at the top of your head and the sides; you are gray everywhere!" I proceeded to explain that I wasn't sure that I wanted to do that anymore, that the process was becoming costly and that I would have to have it corrected frequently. I had thought that maybe it was time to let it go all natural.

I told her that I might be fortunate enough to have inherited my mother's silvery-gray hair and that I thought that it looked really nice on women I had seen. I was going to have to face growing old one day, and after all, I was a grandmother, even if I was only forty-six. She immediately went into a tirade, telling me that I didn't want to do that, that it would be different if I were "petite" and spry. She said that even *she* wouldn't be able to pull off having gray hair—whatever that meant!

I must admit that I was having reservations about whether this was indeed a true friend, although the years had shown me that she was. I was just bouncing back from the news that my insurance company was raising my monthly fees because of high lipids and because of my build. What a sensitive way to say "because you're short and fat"! Good thing that I have a pretty good body image, because when I look in the mirror, I don't see short and fat. That is the blessing of losing your eyesight! As one of my favorite coffee mugs says, "I'm not fat; I'm just short for my weight!" What my friend was now saying was "You don't want to be short and fat and have gray hair!" Horrors.

I left our get-together feeling uplifted and encouraged—not. I actually left confused and wondering why our culture really does seem to run counter to what God says is true. I left wondering whether God really cared about us coloring our hair. I know he knows us so well and cares for us so much that He even knows how many hairs are on our head. "Indeed, the very hairs of your head are all numbered. Don't be afraid; you are worth more than many sparrows." Luke 12: 7 (NIV) If I did decide to reveal my real color to the world, at what age would I decide to do that? What would be the perfect coming-out age? Should I succumb to peer pressure and get rid of the "horrid" gray, or should I let the roots do their thing and chalk it up to experience?

I'd never been much of a follower, so I decided to give it a try. Months later, my hair was almost grown out and I had a stylish little cut. I remained alive and well and not horrified to see what my real color looked like.

I was picking up payroll for our small business just the other day, when our accountant came up to say hello. She greeted me with "Your hair really looks nice!"

I said, "Thanks! I'm letting all my gray come in."

She responded with, "I am too!" There was an instant mutual understanding as we high-fived each other to express that understanding. I told her my concerns and fears of others' opinions, and she said, "When my friends tell me it's going to make me look so much older, I'm going to respond, 'I *am* old!'"

I thank You, Lord, that I don't have to look to our ever-changing culture for approval. I have Your approval, and that is all that really matters.

#JobNotDone

These commandments that I give you today are to
be on your hearts. Impress them on your children.
Talk about them when you sit at home and when
you walk along the road, when you lie down and
when you get up.

—Deuteronomy 6:6–7 (NIV)

I remember, after twenty-two years of parenting under my belt
and with two more children to raise, finding myself with more time
on my hands than I was used to.

I was accustomed to four children and all the busyness associated
with that, and now my responsibilities had been cut in half. I wasn't
sure how to handle this extra time, so I decided to check out some
volunteering opportunities. A director of one of the organizations,
whom I had known for years, even said to me, "Well, you are finally
going to get involved."

I only volunteered for two days that summer before I quit! Our
youngest son kept calling me, wondering when I would be home.
I quickly saw the absurdity of me volunteering when I was clearly
needed at home. He was at an age where I didn't feel needed, but I
was. The problem is that we stay-at-home moms can struggle with
knowing the value of our job. The culture we live in doesn't value it,
and often, especially when our children become more independent,
it seems as though we are not needed. But nothing could be further
from the truth.

I was so glad to see a program aired on which moms got honest
and confessed that they did indeed work because they couldn't take
being at home. They couldn't wait to get away from their children,
and they shared that it was definitely easier and more fulfilling to be
at work. I really appreciated their honesty. The stay-at-home job is
difficult. It can be frustrating at times, and the rewards of our efforts

may not be seen for years. Our American culture has devalued and underestimated the important role that mothers play, and I can't help but think that our nation is suffering because of it.

I know there are circumstances under which moms, especially single-parent moms, don't have a choice but to leave the home to work. This isn't meant to inflict more guilt on those moms but to encourage moms that their role in their children's lives is invaluable.

During this period of time my other son had made some choices that resulted in his vehicle being taken away. Because of his involvement in a program associated with school, I had to reschedule my life to pick him up at 1 p.m. daily, drop him off, and return at 3:30 to pick him up and bring him home. It really hampered my life at this stage. I was finding myself resenting the daily schedule, when a song by Wayne Watson came on the radio, with these lyrics: "At such a time as this, I was placed upon the earth to hear the voice of God and do his will, whatever it is." God is so amazing! He used this artist's gift to make me realize that I was buying into the thinking that doing something significant meant success in the business world or traveling across the world to be a missionary.

I had been praying about what I should do in this new season of life, and God was letting me know, very clearly, that I was right where I was supposed to be. Yes, my job as a wife to my husband and a mother to my two children was where he wanted me for that season.

Granted, by the world's standards it wasn't very glamorous, but I was enjoying some more free time. I took up tennis at this new stage and met a lot of new friends. I even got my youngest son out on the courts. I knew that I was now shaping lives of the future, and I knew I was exactly where God wanted me to be. I was right at home with being right at home!

Lord, forgive me for questioning whether I really am making a difference in the lives of these children You have loaned to me. Your word tells us that our children are a gift from You and You have entrusted them to us. Help me to block out society's idea of success and remind me that bringing home a paycheck isn't an indicator of how valuable this job of raising our children is. Help me to be content with each stage of life that I'm in, not rushing each stage at the risk of missing what You have for me, right where I am.

#LonelyDays

Jesus often withdrew to lonely places and prayed.

–Luke: 5:16 (NIV)

I remember listening to the lyrics of the Three Dog Night song "One." "One is the loneliest, number one is the loneliest, and number one is the loneliest number that you'll ever know. Two can be as bad as one, but the loneliest number is the number one."

Maybe I was affected by that song more than I realized. According to my mom, from a very young age I sought out people to spend time with. She said on summer days I would be up and planning my day around people. Some of my best memories are riding my bike to the school in the summertime, where they offered a craft program and swimming in the neighborhood pool. It seems I would do anything in an effort not to be alone.

Because of this new stage of life that has me and my friends busy with work, home responsibilities, adult children and grandchildren, and aging parents, my friend time feels diminished. I find that doing life a lot on my own just isn't as much fun. My logical husband reminds me that I do spend a large amount of time with people, but he recognizes that it just isn't enough for me.

I'm trying to use this time to develop new interests and learn to enjoy this new phenomena of quiet. I truly find it an adjustment to get used to hearing quiet. With four children, a husband, and a dog, quiet didn't exist! I'd thought I longed for it. I try to remind myself how I couldn't wait for the magazine-lined coffee table, and time to shower, and time to get ready to leave the house without interruptions. I really am coming to understand why we need quietness at this stage of life. Remembering all that we have to remember becomes more difficult, and fewer distractions are helpful. I had that experience this week again, as I hid a piece of jewelry so well I couldn't locate it!

I recently dropped in on a friend, the kind of friend you feel comfortable just dropping in on without warning. She was curled up in a chair with her blanket and her little dachshund perched above her head. She was reading and savoring the quiet. We discussed this new stage, and I found she had a much more positive reaction to it than I did. We have the kind of friendship in which you can be in the same room and be comfortable with silence. She said at one point, "Can you hear how quiet my house is? Isn't it wonderful?" I told her I was actually struggling with it. I was trying to learn to enjoy it, but often it was much too quiet for my liking. Another benefit of friendship is working together through the changes that come with the different seasons of life.

One afternoon when I was caught up with everything at home, I decided to go to see a movie that I had heard was good. I ordered my popcorn and a drink, and I felt like a little kid in a candy shop when I realized that I didn't have to share! Being a bit early, I meandered into the theater and chose a seat toward the back and in the middle. From there I people-watched as the theater began to fill. It was a chick flick, so I saw several women friends stroll in together, then an older couple, and then another single woman choosing her seat. It was a matinee, so the theater wasn't that full, but even so there were three of us who were alone.

I was talking to a neighbor that night, and I told her that I had gone by myself. She informed me that she had never gone to a movie by herself. Another divorced friend told me that in her divorce-care group one of their assignments had been to go to a movie alone and eat a meal out alone. Hmm, maybe I wasn't that weird and this was a healthy step for me. I've done very little in my life alone. Maybe this was my discovery time.

Thank You, Lord, for walking with me through every new season of life. Seasons may at times feel uncertain and lonely, but help me learn to enjoy each stage and discover what You have for me in this new life!

#NotCool

If we claim we have no sin, we are only fooling ourselves and not living in the truth. But if we confess our sins to him, he is faithful and just to forgive us our sins and to cleanse us from all wickedness. If we claim we have not sinned, we are calling God a liar and showing that his word has no place in our hearts.

—1 John 1:8–10 (NLT)

My husband and I stopped at a hotel for a night on the way home from a visit with our son. As we were packing up the next morning to head home, we heard all kinds of obscenities being spewed from the other side of the thin walls. We weren't sure whether it was a husband and wife or a parent and child. As we walked out to head for breakfast, we realized two teenage girls were the recipients of the rage. They were sitting by the pool like two whipped puppies, and the mom had a scowl on her face.

There was a time when I would have stood in judgment of that mother. I couldn't have imagined a mother speaking to her children like that. While it was still very wrong, I have experienced frustration in parenting that revealed the sin in my heart like nothing else could have. So I prayed for this mom and for her daughters. I prayed that the daughters would come to know their value in Christ and that the words out of their mother's mouth wouldn't scar them. I prayed that the mom would have a desire to apologize for the words she'd spewed out in anger.

Have you ever had one of those days when you are up to your ears in demands, and then something else unexpected comes along and sends you over the edge? I had more than one of these when my children were teens, and it wasn't a pretty picture.

I had experienced lots of things with my four children, but one thing I hadn't faced yet as a parent was having a child in jail. My eldest son had made some careless driving decisions, two in one day, and the high school police officer had decided that he had enough and taken him to jail. If that wasn't enough pressure, our other son had procrastinated on a high school paper and needed help to get this finished by the following morning.

We'd always said that if a child of ours ended up in jail by his own fault we would not bail him out. Well, we discovered that if we didn't, he would be in there for almost a month, until his hearing, and we didn't want to jeopardize his graduation because of too many absences.

When my husband brought our son home from jail that evening, I started to talk about it, and he told me he wanted to drop it. I didn't want to drop it. He then tried to minimize the entire situation, and that did it. Have you ever felt that you have tried really hard as a parent, that you have given up over twenty years of your life to make parenting a priority, and then you get something like this? That was my frame of mind, and I went into You-don't-think-this-is-a-big-deal mode and decided to shock my family into recognizing my frustration. I walked into the kitchen, grabbed a dinner plate, and purposefully threw it with all my might onto the tile floor, watching it shatter into a million pieces. I then went into a Tourette's syndrome routine, using every word that I could think of that I'd taught my children not to use. I told you it wasn't pretty. I also—which is what I'm most ashamed of—proceeded to use my Lord's name in vain. I haven't discerned yet why that is what spewed forth from my tongue, except that in my heart I was angry at my circumstances and apparently blaming God for allowing this entire situation. But more simply and more accurately, it was my sin coming out.

After that I swept up the destruction that I had caused, and then my husband and I worked together to start cleaning up the emotional destruction, which proved to be much harder. The one who had gone to jail left the house in anger, to stay with a friend, and we talked through things with our youngest son.

Dear Heavenly Father, Thank You for allowing me to see the depth of my sin. Thank You for taking on the punishment that I deserve and for allowing me to see where I fall short. When I now see such blatant sins in others, I am able to be more compassionate and less and less judgmental, knowing that I am capable of the same. Thank You for telling Your people that you came not to call the righteous but the sinners. Thank You for enabling us to come to you and confess and for being faithful to forgive us from all unrighteousness.

#Oorah

Be strong. Take courage. Don't be intimidated.
Don't give them a second thought because God,
your God, is striding ahead of you. He's right there
with you. He won't let you down; he won't leave you.

—Deuteronomy 31:6 (MSG)

After almost a year, I was just beginning to see progress with my adjustment to our firstborn's leaving the nest when he came home for a visit with two fellow marines.

The "men" were in and out, thoroughly enjoying their ninety-six-hour freedom. They were out at the moment, so I went back to a neighborhood project of passing out a newsletter. I stopped by the house to get a drink and to use the bathroom facilities.

As I sat there, quietly minding my own business, I heard that old familiar cry of "Mo-o-om" echo throughout the house. I chose to ignore it, because I had tried to teach the kids to look for me first rather than yelling my name. I'd also taught them to knock before entering. Knowing the unique cries of my four children, I discerned that this was not an emergency cry.

I sat still, trying to ignore his pleas for my response. I contemplated how for the past twelve months I had struggled with the idea that my job was done and how I would have loved to hear that familiar voice. *He has been on his own,* I told myself, *and made it crystal clear that he is independent of us.* This was my opportunity to prove my independence from him!

The cry of Mom! resounded in the direction of our bedroom door and into the larger bathroom area beyond my closed door. "Mom! I've been looking everywhere for you! Why haven't you answered me?" He would have been a good candidate for drill sergeant!

I was ready. I calmly responded with "_____," I am in the bathroom; can what you have to say to me please wait until I am finished?" He gave me the affirmative, upon which I finished with my business.

A few minutes later I walked through the living room, where he and his two fellow marines were waiting for me to speak to him. And kids say parents embarrass them!

"Mom, can we take the Mustang to the beach?"

"I'm sorry, but I asked you not to smoke in the car, and I noticed a cigarette burn on the floor mat. I'll see you guys later; I'm going to finish delivering these newsletters."

I picked the newsletters up and continued around our block. I felt like the bad guy, but I *knew* that I had made the right decision. It didn't feel cool being the adult at that moment. It felt very lonely, but I reminded myself that my son needed a parent right now, not another friend. I chuckled to think that he was all grown up in some ways and could even fight for our country but was still knocking on my bathroom door!

Lord, I thank You for how far you have brought me through this past year with letting go of the first child You loaned to us.

Thank you for the stamina and courage to mother and father this strong-willed child.

#StatusChange

Children's children are a crown to the aged."

—Proverbs 17:6 (NIV)

Only approximately one week left, and my title of *mother* will be expanded to include *grandmother*. Now, don't get me wrong. I'm eager to meet this new little person, but I would be lying if I didn't admit that with the title comes a bit of trepidation.

First of all, can you believe no one involved me in this decision to make me a grandmother? I had absolutely no deciding vote in whether I was ready be a grandmother! I should have learned by now that I have absolutely no control over anything, but it isn't an easy lesson to learn!

The extra weight I'm carrying and the gray hairs that are showing and the soft lap that I'm getting should have been a warning that I was getting close! And when my teens pointed out that the hairs on my chin were scaring them and that my makeup wasn't applied quite right, and I realize that this is because my sight has started to take a turn for the worse, I should have known.

When I told my son, about to become a new father, that I had finished up a cross-stitch piece for the baby and that it had nearly blinded me doing it, he responded in a patronizing way: "Mom, be careful." I should have known! This was the child who, a few short years ago, had suggested I give up parenting and get a "real job"!

Yes, the signs are all there, and I'm even starting to say, "But I feel like I'm sixteen on the inside"—especially when the "oldies" are on the radio. That's another big clue! And when I'm laughing with my son on the phone about potty-training stories, and he tells me to be careful or I'll wet myself, reality is starting to kick in.

What does growing old gracefully mean, anyway? How am I going to do this, Lord? I know, I know, one day at a time. You'll show me. You haven't let me down yet.

Thank you, Lord, for the gift of grandchildren. Even though it may not have been in my timing, they truly are a gift.

#StormAlert

> Your God, to whom you are so loyal, is going to get
> you out of this.
>
> —Daniel 6:16 (MSG)

I was reluctantly taking a walk one morning. I use the word *reluctantly* because I am anything but a walking enthusiast. But since I know it is good for my health, I'm trying to learn to be. I pushed myself this particular morning and went a bit further than my usual turning-around point so that I could work up to a three-mile routine.

As I walked, it started to sprinkle and then it stopped. Then it started coming down pretty steadily, and I started wondering whether my husband, who was working at home in his office, would ever notice that it was raining and come to my rescue.

I tried to enjoy the feeling of the rain on my head and as it hit my face. I started wondering why people worked so hard at trying to get out of the rain. When it starts to rain, people start running to shelters, covering themselves with whatever they can find: purses, newspapers, coats and, if they are prepared people, umbrellas and raincoats. I was trying to enjoy the moment and the coolness of the rain, but honestly I kept watching each car that went around the bend to see whether it was my husband coming to give me a lift. I started picking up my pace to get to my desired destination, home!

When it became obvious that I was not going to be rescued, my mind started wandering, as it often does, and I started thinking of how this might apply to our lives. None of us like storms in our lives. We can count on the storms to come; we are told not to be surprised by them. We would like the storms to stop, but since we can't control them, we try to avoid them, run from them, or hope to be rescued from them. You'd think we would've learned by now that, hard as we might try, they can't be avoided. We can't outrun the storms, so why can't we just acknowledge that they will come and be prepared?

By *prepared* I mean that we should know by now that the storms will bring about good in our lives. While I hated being in the storms, I can say that after a storm (not always immediately) I could see how it had changed me.

I met a young mother this week for the first time and started asking her questions about her life. I guess I asked the wrong question—or the right one. When I inquired about her husband and his work, she burst into tears and ran out of the room. Unbeknownst to me, her husband had been out of work for some time, and I opened a flood of emotion and tears. She later apologized to me through someone else, which wasn't necessary. Apologize for tears? It must be that water thing again. Crying has health benefits. But why are we so afraid to let someone see our tears? Like rain, tears were designed for our good; they release stress hormones.

As I rounded the corner to my street, there was Johnny-come-lately, looking down the street to see if I needed rescuing! Chuckling when he saw how wet I was, he apologized for not noticing in time.

How can we get to the point where we stop running from them and learn to see God's hand in the storms? Can't we trust Him to use them to make us more like Him? I don't know whether we will ever be able to actually welcome storms, but as we go through them, maybe we can encourage one another that we will come out the other side in one piece. We can look forward to the day when we arrive safely at our real home, where the storms will be no more, where there is warmth and light and safety and no more sin.

Lord, I thank You that You promised to never leave or forsake us and that, unlike my husband who has been my faithful companion for thirty-eight years, You will not become preoccupied and forget about me but will come to my rescue!

#TableTalk

Give us today our daily bread

—Matthew 6:11 (NIV)

I joined my father-in-law and three of his companions for dinner at his assisted living facility one evening.

He was the only man at the table; it was him and, including me, four women. As I met the women individually and learned their names, I found it intriguing to learn about their personal lives.

The one woman said she had only been at this new home for a few weeks and had just celebrated her 101st birthday! She was as "sharp as a tack," as my mom would say, and actually looked younger than her companions who were in their eighties. I asked her what she attributed her longevity to, and she said she had no idea. "I guess the Lord isn't finished with me yet!"

The next woman had taken on the job of mothering my father-in-law. She asked me whether I knew that a pair of his shoes had been stolen! Knowing that they had been thrown out because they had holes in the soles and that his new ones weren't being worn, I explained to her that there wasn't a thief in his building. She was glad to learn that I was up with what was going on. She asked me if I would write my phone number down so that she could contact me if there were any other situations with Dad. I learned that after her husband had died she'd had no intentions to remarry but that a persistent gentlemen suitor had talked her into it. She explained that she was a widow now for the second time.

The third woman at the table, whom I only knew as Rose, had

all she could do to concentrate on eating. She would lean over and whisper to the woman next to her when she needed something, and we would all try to help her out by summoning a waiter. She had nothing to say during the entire meal.

One by one the women finished and left the table, leaving the one I had learned nothing about except her name. She started to rise and went to look for her walker, only to find that someone had taken hers by mistake. I comforted her by telling her that I would let the staff at the desk know so that she could locate her own walker. As I started to leave, she grabbed me by the hand and quietly told me how much she'd enjoyed having me at her table. She then explained that she was legally blind and couldn't hear very well, so it was hard for her to participate in the conversation, but she'd enjoyed my presence at her table. She went on to explain that she'd sensed that everyone had enjoyed themselves and that though she couldn't hear the conversation she had heard and enjoyed the laughter.

I was amazed that somehow I had made a difference in this woman's life, if only for a few moments. But I was more amazed at the way God had used this woman to encourage me. I couldn't help but think how appropriately she was named.

Thank You, Lord, for the encouragement You bring at the most unexpected times.

CHAPTER 9

UNCONDITIONAL LOVE

#AttitudeShift

You will go out in joy and be led forth in peace; the
mountains and hills will burst into song before you.
And all the trees of the field will clap their hands.

—Isaiah 55:12 (NIV)

I found myself turning down an invitation to a special women's
program, even after some precious pleading from a dear friend.
Instead I went to visit my father-in-law at his retirement home. As
I arrived, I caught him about to enter the social hall for a special
dancing program. Providence obviously had it that I would be
attending a program one way or another.

I was feeling overwhelmed with life and all the responsibilities
that go along with it. I had been gathering tax information for us,
our business, two of our sons, and my father-in-law. He had just
gotten out of the hospital for an infected hand that had been cut in
a show of temper in his dining room. Our nineteen-year-old had just
wrecked another car, and my mom was unhappy about my father's
health problems. I was just feeling grumpy and certainly didn't feel
like attending an event where I had to put on a smile even when I
didn't feel like it.

As I entered the room, I saw many different faces, each telling a
different story. A lady who seemed to know my father-in-law walked

toward us and asked if the seat was taken next to me; a hat had been thrown on the seat. I told her a man had laid it there but as far as I was concerned she could sit there. I asked her how long she had lived there, and she told me six months. When I asked her if she liked it, she said, "No!" She said she had her own house, but her kids thought she needed to "retire." I asked her whether she was meeting new friends, and she said not really, that most of the people there were much older than she was. I tried to point out the positive things about her new home in hopes of encouraging her, but it seemed to no avail. I think she was having a day like mine!

The man who had laid the hat on the chair came over to give my neighbor what-for about removing his hat and taking his seat. She told him she didn't think that reserving seats was allowed, and he went off in a huff.

Another couple squeezed between our chairs to get a back-row seat. When there weren't two seats for him and his wife, the wife went over to find a seat across the room. We attempted to find two seats together, but he retorted, "I've been married for years! Why would I care if I didn't sit with her tonight!"

People continued to wander in, and they needed a staff member to referee while they all jockeyed for the seats they desired.

I watched faces as we waited. Some were wearing pleasant smiles and others donning grumpy faces and negative attitudes to go along with them. I watched and speculated on what each of their lives was like. I wondered what they were thinking tonight as they came to watch this show. I pondered what type of person I would be when and if I reached that age. Then I reflected that I had been pretty grumpy myself lately and that it was time to work on an attitude adjustment. I also thought how nice it was to be in a place where I didn't have to pretend. These people were being themselves, and if you didn't like it, you could take a big fat leap.

The entertainment turned out to be a couple in their sixties who danced—and could they dance! I watched the frowns turn to smiles and laughs, the hands started to clap, and the feet start to tap. The bickering stopped while for some forty-five minutes everyone enjoyed the colorful costumes, the movement, the music, and the jokes. For a few minutes all the cares of the world were put aside, and they all shared the universal love of music and dancing.

Thank You, Lord, for loving us even when we are unlovable and for giving different gifts to different people that can be used to bring joy and encouragement to others. Thanks for helping us get through some very difficult days, and thanks for the man who told me that every day we have a choice to be either a sweet pickle or a sour pickle. Help me to turn to You, so I won't be of the sour variety!

#FoldsofLove

Our children and their children will get in on this
as the word is passed along from parent to child.
Babies not yet conceived will hear the good news
— that God does what he says.

—Psalm 22:30–31 (MSG)

When my husband and I were newlyweds, we didn't have a washer and dryer in our married-student housing townhouse, so we would take our laundry across the street to the laundromat in our community. In the winters we would often be tramping through cold, wet snow before entering the warmth of the building.

I'm not sure how it got started, but as we took our bedsheets out of the dryer, we would stand apart from each other to make the folds and when we went to fold it in half we would walk toward each other with the sheets between us, embrace, and give each other a big bear hug! I'm sure the cold Indiana winters and the warmth of the sheets inspired us!

We continued this tradition while raising our children, and they would automatically do it when we were folding sheets or blankets together.

Our grandchildren were visiting recently, and they are now old enough to be quite the helpers. As I started to fold a blanket, one of my grandsons rushed over to help me. As we went through the steps, he automatically went in for the hug! My granddaughter was observing, and her response brought joy to my heart: "That's how we fold sheets at our house!"

I was so excited to think that this tradition had been passed on to the third generation!

Lord, thank You for the encouragement that our children did pick up, not just our weaknesses but our strengths as well. We never claimed perfection, but we tried to point them to the One who exemplified perfection. You know our prayer and the desire of our hearts would be for all of our children and grandchildren to be in the fold of your perfect love.

#GentleGiant

Train up a child in the way he should go, Even when he is old he will not depart from it.

—Proverbs 22:6 (NASB)

Letting a child go is never easy and doesn't often come without tears, but there are circumstances that are beyond the routine goodbye to your child as he or she is dropped off to go to college or move into his own place.

I had the privilege and pain of glimpsing what one mother and father had to experience as they released their youngest son at the young age of fifteen. Ryan was born in 1982. He was diagnosed with autism at the age of two. I didn't meet Ryan until he was a teen. I met his mom at a women's luncheon as she was sharing with someone about a new communication tool for her and her son. I was curious about this thing called autism, and I was drawn to this mother's hope for her child. Our friendship began there.

It is difficult to put into words what this family's daily life was like. Ryan was nicknamed by his family a "gentle giant." His mom and dad knew him as a gentle, loving son. But because of his size, 6 foot, 230 pounds, along with some of the self-stimulatory behaviors of autism, like "stemming" (which is a rocking-back-and-forth motion) and his inability to make direct eye contact, he could be intimidating. His mom would so often say that he was misunderstood by the world. You see, Ryan was completely nonverbal, and he would understandably become frustrated and act out.

Ryan's behavior escalated when he hit puberty, and after a few dangerous situations when he put himself and others in harm's way, the school administrators came to the conclusion that they didn't have a place for Ryan. Thus he was placed into a residential facility about three and a half hours away from his family.

There are some similarities about normal goodbyes. You know your children are growing up, you know they have to do things that aren't going to be easy, and you fear how the world will treat them. But can you imagine sending a child away whom you have personally loved and taken care of for fifteen years and he isn't able to even express to you how he feels? He can't even say the word goodbye.

I attended a going-away party for Ryan. He loved it. Ryan loves cake and punch and balloons as much as any other kid, and he knew he was loved that night, as family and friends surrounded him with lots of love, fellowship, and hugs.

His parents headed up the next day and did the hardest thing they'd ever had to do; they dropped Ryan off and said goodbye. I spent time with his mom during the first three weeks after he was gone. What a roller coaster of emotions! It made menopause look like a breeze. Was she enjoying the freedom? You bet. Was her heart breaking? Of course.

Three weeks later, the time came for her first visit. They invited me to go along with them and spend a couple of nights, as her husband had to go back to work. As we got closer and closer I could feel Ryan's mom's anticipation; she was about to see her baby!

As we opened the car door, his behavior specialist came walking out with him. He had the biggest grin on his face and immediately started expressing his love by kissing his mom and dad, something they had taught him and which was giving them indescribable joy at this moment. I am crying as I type this, as the emotion of that moment was so simultaneously beautiful and painful. We all knew that this reunion would end in yet another painful goodbye.

You could tell Ryan was loving this visit. People can care about you, but no one loves you and knows you like your parents. We took a picnic to a park and walked the boardwalk with Ryan. We looked at his room, and his mom made plans to personalize it for him; a stark room with bare walls wouldn't do.

The time came to return to our room for the evening. I saw her agonize as she prepared to say goodbye and tell Ryan that we would see him the next day. She didn't want him to think she was gone for good again, for fear he would get upset and have to be restrained for acting out. As we approached the car, the sniffles turned into sobs and then the sobs into torrents. I felt her pain but did not know how to comfort her. All I could do was tell her she had to let it out. I, too, had cried like that over my son's leaving, and I knew that the grief had to be released. Her husband, who was driving back that night, had gone. He had not cried, but I knew that his pain was every bit as deep. I empathized for him, thinking of his long ride back home, alone. I ached to think that they both were feeling their pain so deeply and that they weren't able to comfort each other.

As we sat outside talking about her feelings, she just kept sobbing, "My heart has been yanked out." I just listened and prayed.

I prayed that night that the next day would be easier. I prayed that this mom would be comforted and that she could experience peace in the midst of this horror. I prayed that this was indeed the right place for her son to be. I prayed that, if this wasn't the right thing to do, she would sense that as well. After little sleep that night, we returned to the school to work through Ryan's educational plan.

The meeting went well, and we took Ryan out for lunch and a walk. He typed on his board by pointing to the letters that he was "sad." His mom bravely told him that his feelings were okay and that she understood them but that it was time for him to learn new things at his new school. He then typed "go home." She assured him that he would get to come home for visits. He then asked where his dad and brother were, and she explained that they'd had to stay home to work.

She didn't tell him that her heart was breaking or that everything in her being was telling her that this all seemed so wrong. This mom, in my mind, deserved a purple heart; she exhibited courage similar to that of a beribboned soldier. She did it tearlessly, something that I knew was only possible because of the strength she was receiving from her Heavenly Father.

We finished the day taking care of details, and then it was time to head out. We hugged Ryan and told him we liked his new school. His teacher asked him for help carrying some things, and we turned around and walked out. We got in the car, and Ryan's mom said, "I'm not crying!" I couldn't believe it: "I'm not crying!" This mom had cleared the next hurdle of her letting-go process, and she'd accomplished it first class!

Dear Heavenly Father, thank You for walking with my friends through this painful process of letting their son go. I pray that you will give Ryan's parents your peace as they begin this new stage of life, which will be much different than the last fifteen years of their lives. Thank You for their example of perseverance and for giving them commitment to their marriage in the midst of some extremely trying situations. Thank You for the unconditional love, sacrifice, and dedication they have shown and continue to demonstrate to their "gentle giant." I have learned much about your attributes from watching them.

#GottaLuvMaleMind

Better a dry crust with peace and quiet than a house
full of feasting with strife.

—Proverbs 17:1 (NLT)

I awakened on a Friday morning and decided to fix my husband
a bacon-and-egg breakfast before he left for work. I knew that a good
breakfast would be a good start to his day after a grueling work week.

Our youngest son stopped by to talk to his dad about some
business things, so I offered him an egg as well. As they were talking,
I was looking for my salt and pepper shakers and remembered that
they were out on the table in the back room. I asked my husband if
he would please grab the shakers.

A few seconds later he re-entered the kitchen—with two
television remotes in his hand, which he laid down by the frying pan!
I asked him why he was bringing the remotes to me and where he
had placed the shakers. He chuckled as he realized that he had been
distracted and had picked up the remotes. Our system takes two
remotes; one is black and one is white! He really hadn't been trying
to be funny. He'd just headed out for them while continuing his
conversation with our son, and his mind had seen black and white,
salt and pepper. Obvious! And I wonder why I can't understand
the male brain! My son, who was observing the entire scenario, was
laughing and totally relating to my husband, agreeing that this was
a natural mistake. I was thinking, *We need some more baby girls in
this family!*

The following weekend we were talking to a waitress who was
asking my husband all kinds of questions: "Do you put the lid on
the toothpaste tube?"

My husband responded, "We don't buy those anymore; we buy
the squirt type."

"Do you put your dirty clothes in the hamper, or do you drop them where you take them off?"

I was just enjoying the conversation and being entertained by my husband's responses. If she only knew the beginning of what you'll put up with in each other when you're in love!

I thank You, Lord, that after thirty-eight years of marriage I have learned to overlook the things that really don't matter and dwell on traits that I originally fell in love with! I thank You too that we went into this institution of marriage knowing that there would be differences but committed to not allowing them to become deal breakers. Thanks for giving me a husband who has been committed to me and loved me for who I am, idiosyncrasies and all!

#LooneyTimes

If any of you lacks wisdom, you should ask God, who gives generously to all without finding fault, and it will be given to you. But when you ask, you must believe and not doubt, because the one who doubts is like a wave of the sea, blown and tossed by the wind. That person should not expect to receive anything from the Lord. Such a person is double-minded and unstable in all they do.

—James 1:5–6 (NIV)

The teen years can be challenging and exasperating; they have been known to drive the parents absolutely crazy! Our experience has been that the crazy behavior climaxes during the last year of high school. I guess this isn't a new phenomenon, as this behavior has been dubbed *senioritis*. It doesn't make it any easier to know that it is common. The cold is common too, but it isn't something that I look forward to, and I will do my best to avoid it!

I believe that sharing our difficult times in life can help others to not feel so alone. Thus I will share some of our "senior" stories. I guess the fact that my husband and I are going through this now for the third time, a little bit closer to receiving senior's benefits ourselves, makes these trials even harder. We are just plain discouraged and downright weary.

Our son wanted to drive up to look at a college that he and a friend were considering. Since he would soon be nineteen and we knew that he would be leaving in just a couple short months, we thought this was reasonable. While on their way home, they spotted a deer—that is, a four-legged deer—and apparently the desire to go after it became irresistible, and all sense of logic went out the door.

Because we live in a rural area, his buddy had a hunting rifle in the car, so our son jumped out of the truck with the gun and hopped a fence. And who happened to be passing by? None other than a wildlife officer! My son was arrested for armed trespassing, since he was on private property, and put in jail for five hours. We never did know about it until after he was out of jail. He had told his buddy that his parents wouldn't bail him out, since he had already used up his one get-out-of-jail card for reckless driving—so his friend's mother did! I'm always amazed at parents who choose to make decisions without contacting the other parents, but at this phase of my life I'm just glad we didn't have to deal with it. She bailed him out, and she can wait to be repaid.

After questioning our son about his decision, we discussed the consequences and the plans he had for facing what could be a felony charge. This was the son who had gone to hunter's education courses since he was small and who later, as a teen, had been a counselor at a youth camp and helped teach hunters' education! Since he was eighteen, he decided that "he" would hire a lawyer.

A couple of days later, in the middle of all of this, my husband called while I was sitting in a doctor's office addressing invitations to an open house for our son's high school graduation. He had just received a call from a dean at the school, letting us know that our son had decided to skip class and go work out in the gym—and do a little "chew" while pumping iron. Does this make any sense? Pump my body up, and rot the inside of my mouth out. We were talking three weeks until he was out of high school for good—and he couldn't just follow the rules for a few more days?

My husband and I decided we badly needed to get out alone, so we went out for dinner, leaving our sixteen-year-old, our fourth and last child, to finish repainting a boat that he and his dad were restoring. We had a nice dinner, and the pounding in our heads had ceased. Then, when we pulled back onto our street, we saw our sixteen-year-old, who had a beginner's permit, pulling into our driveway with a buddy!

I rolled down the window and yelled, "What do you think you're doing?" I was starting to feel that there had been absolutely no brains passed down from me or my husband at all!

His way of describing his feelings: "I'm feeling dumber by the minute by just watching what is going on!" The car had been across the street at a neighbor's to avoid overspray, and he had been driving it back and forth while we were there as the boat was being worked on. But he had decided, since we weren't around, to just drive it to the end of our long street. My husband and I have always found it uncanny how our children can't do anything without us finding out about it. That has been a prayer of ours, one that I may reconsider. I believe denial might be an easier way to live!

In trying to come up with a punishment to fit the crime, I told him to head into the computer room and type something about what he'd done, why he had done it, and what the results could have been of what he had chosen to do.

Sorry! I was going to put the car in the driveway and just went a little further and I know I was wrong and it won't happen ever again. What could happen is I could have hit someone and hurt my friend, and I put myself in danger and if a cop would have saw me they would have called mom and dad. I do know what I was thinking. I am stressed out, just like you, and I just did it without thinking.

And I just felt really stupid for what I did, and if there is any way you can forgive me, please do, and I am so SORRY! Love, _____

Of all things, the day was Mother's Day! In spite of all that had happened, that day was going to be about me. The mother of three sons and a daughter, I was going to celebrate Mother's Day—and my husband and I were escaping! Some young married friends without children joked about us going away. Didn't most mothers want to be with their children on Mother's Day? They even asked our youngest son how he felt about his mom going away on Mother's Day. He responded, "I think they both need it." He was right. Then he asked, "You're taking my keys?"

Lord, thank You for a soul mate who is there to help me walk through getting these children raised. Thank You for humor and for giving us rest at night so we can start a new day with all the trials from the previous day put into perspective. Thank You for walking with us and giving us wisdom, one step at a time.

#NotOnTodaysList

Answering before listening is both stupid and rude.

—Proverbs 18:13 (MSG)

It was my day off, and I had a list which I planned to knock down as best I could in a day. Then one of my sons stopped by the house; he was going to do some work for us. He came inside to say hi and, I discerned from past experience, possibly to get a bite to eat. Single and twenty-five, he was not much into preparing meals, I knew, and I had told him he was welcome to stop by anytime to get a bite to eat out of our refrigerator.

Knowing food speaks to the hearts of men, I asked him if he had time for me to fix him some bacon and eggs. He said he would take the time. He then proceeded to unload a plethora of words in an effort to express his frustrations with his chosen career and some difficulties he was experiencing in dealing with people. I wasn't prepared for all that I was hearing; it certainly hadn't been on my list for the day. This particular son was typically so upbeat, too, so this seemed out of character. It felt as if he were dumping his anger on me.

I'd thought the fact that I had stopped long enough to fix his breakfast would have been enough sacrifice, but apparently it was not. He continued to run past me all of his thoughts, along with a few expletives. I quickly realized that he wasn't wanting any advice from me but just a place to vent. But I didn't really feel like listening. I felt inadequate in knowing how to respond to the hopelessness he was feeling. Because of his demeanor, I finally made the decision to tell him that I had things to do. I started down my list by making a phone call I needed to make. When he saw that I was done talking, he got up and headed out the door, telling me sorry as he exited.

I finished my phone call and started praying. "Lord, I don't know what is really going on with him. I don't know how to help him or even how to encourage him. Please put someone in his life who he can talk to and who will encourage him." I turned back to my list, and in a few minutes my son was back at the front door to apologize. I continued to pray for him during the day, and my husband and I prayed together for him the next morning. The following afternoon he stopped by—yes, to fix a quick bite. Knowing he had gone to a young adult program at church the previous night, I asked him if he'd heard anything encouraging to him. He said yes. Wasn't that always the way it worked? And he pulled out an outline of the lesson from his pocket and shared it with me.

Thank You, Lord, for loving my son even more than I am capable of and for reminding me that You who started a good work in him are faithful to finish what You started! Thanks, too, for others who love You and out of gratitude to You for changing their hearts are investing in his life. Thank You for Your word and its power to change hearts and lives.

#OnOneKnee

> Husbands, go all out in your love for your wives, exactly as Christ did for the church — a love marked by giving, not getting. Christ's love makes the church whole. His words evoke her beauty. Everything he does and says is designed to bring the best out of her, dressing her in dazzling white silk, radiant with holiness. And that is how husbands ought to love their wives.
>
> —Ephesians 5:25–27 (MSG)

I went to my local nail salon on a Friday afternoon to get a pedicure. My neighbor was planning to meet me there. As a roomful of women were pampering themselves, a young man came in to buy a gift certificate for his girlfriend.

Because he was talking loud enough for others to hear, you could see the women, including myself, eavesdropping as he explained why he was purchasing this gift. He began to explain that he would be going on a cruise with his parents and the rest of his family. At the celebration of his parents' twentieth anniversary, he was going to propose to his girlfriend. All the women began to look at one another with grins on their faces as they listened in to how this young man planned to propose.

Being the extrovert that he was, the man noticed that he had the attention of the women in the salon, and so he continued to share his story with all of us. At one point in his story he asked if he could practice his proposal speech on us, to see what we all thought. We were all loving it! He explained that he was giving her this as a gift. His girlfriend had never had a pedicure, and he hoped she would like it, because she had mentioned that she felt funny about the idea of someone else touching her feet. He wondered whether he was making a mistake with this gift, and everyone assured him that she would indeed learn to love it. He might even regret having introduced her to the idea!

He said that he had gotten permission from his parents to propose at their celebration, as he didn't want to take away from their special day. His brother was going to be in on the surprise as well. On the night of the formal dinner and celebration of their parents' anniversary, his brother was going to suggest toasting their parents. After that, he would get up and tell his parents that he admired them for their commitment to each other and express how he desired to have the same kind of commitment and that the only way he could do this was to ask his girl to marry him! At that point he was going to get on his knees and pop the question. There wasn't a dry eye in the place!

As he concluded his story, he looked at all of us in his boyish way and asked, "What do you think?" Everyone assured him that she would love the proposal and encouraged him to continue with his surprises years after they were married. This young man's enthusiasm and love for his girlfriend exuded from him, and it overflowed to all of us. It was the kind of fairy-tale love story that girls dream of, and that roomful of women relived those dreams that day. We all know marriage isn't easy and that not every marriage has a fairy-tale ending. But we also know that working at marriage is worth it and that true love is a decision, a decision to put your mate before yourself, even when you don't feel like it. I hoped this young man would continue with his selfless love and enthusiasm and stay committed to washing the feet of the bride of his youth through whatever life brought their way.

God describes His people as a bride and Himself as the bridegroom. I'm thankful for the word picture this young man gave that day to all of us fortunate enough to be at that salon at that moment. This young man could not have known how he was reminding us of the depth of love God has for us.

God made a decision to love us with an everlasting love. Earthly relationships may fail, but the love of the Father is not merely a fantasy or a dream. It is something we can count on!

Lord, in a culture where it seems couples are lacking endurance in their commitment to each other, I thank You that You have promised to never leave us or forsake us. I pray that this man I met today will hold unswervingly in his love for his new bride. Lord, though earthly husbands may leave or die, You remain faithful to the abandoned and the widows.

#Trustworthy

> You can be sure that God will take care of everything
> you need, his generosity exceeding even yours in the
> glory that pours from Jesus.

—Philippians 4:19 (MSG)

Children have a way of slowing us down—actually, they demand it of us, and I'm learning to be thankful that they do.

My youngest child, my eleven-year-old, has slowed me down a lot this year and opened up a whole new world of contentedness for me. Perhaps because he is the youngest of four, he has discerned that I needed to slow down as he's watched me deal with the other three, in their teens. Maybe he sensed my lack of peace.

This son has always had a love of the outdoors. Fishing and hunting with his dad and brothers sparked this interest. He mastered the art of throwing a fishing net at a very young age and often spent his afternoons whiling away the time catching bait fish in our man-made lake.

One afternoon a green heron flew into our backyard. My son had just caught some bait fish, so he threw some to the bird and watched as he ate it. This continued for quite a few days, and then one evening we were outside and "his" bird flew up on top of the pool screen enclosure, awaiting his dinner. My son told me that he called the bird to be fed and that the bird responded. I waited and watched, and sure enough, this bird answered his call and hovered around until the bait fish were caught and thrown to him!

This went on for months, and each time the bird would walk a little closer to receive his provision. I was amazed that this bird, who was free to fly anywhere, chose to end up in our back yard every day at about the same time! I watched him sit in the palm tree, watching my son as he threw the net and emptied the contents onto the grass. My son then sat very still on the grass and tossed the fish about a foot from himself. I watched the bird just sit and stare for a while and then inch a hair closer, still watching my son to see if he could be trusted, ready to take flight at any second if it became necessary. He kept creeping closer until he finally took the last step to receive his sustenance.

As I watched, I couldn't help but think of how I responded to our God, the great provider. I have so often wanted to trust but found it difficult. I have looked around for my provisions to come from elsewhere. I, too, have doubted whether my God really loves me enough to meet my needs. I saw God in my son's relationship to this bird. He meant no harm to this bird. A dove in a dove field in season, yes—but not this bird on this day. He had every intention of making sure the fish got to the bird. This bird was totally safe, but past experiences had him wary, probably for good reason. He didn't know that my son was totally trustworthy and harmless to him and had his best interest in mind.

Thank You, Lord, for being the greatest provider and for always meeting my needs—not necessarily the *wants* that I think I need! Thanks for loving me and for Your incredible patience with me while I creep toward you, wanting to trust but finding myself doubting.

CHAPTER 10

PROMISED LIFE TO COME

#AllTooMuch

I've told you all this so that trusting me, you will be unshakable and assured, deeply at peace. In this godless world you will continue to experience difficulties. But take heart! I've conquered the world.

—John 16:33 (MSG)

I finally had a day off from my care-giving job and was looking forward to catching up with my own domestic chores. I planned to change sheets and make some necessary but dreaded phone calls that I had been putting off.

I really needed a break, because with my type of job it is easy to take on the physical and mental pain of the people that I am caring for. This particular couple had been married sixty-six years, and recently my job had been to help her get ready and drive her to the rehabilitation facility so she could visit with her husband. He had been experiencing a lot of back pain, which was why he was there. The pain was preventing him from even being able to stand up and walk, so he was not able to stay in his own home. She had been hospitalized herself after experiencing breathing problems, which they determined had been brought on by the stress.

The last day I worked, his bride was a bit discouraged to see him feeling down, and she spoke a little of how hard life could get. She understood that her husband was ninety-three and it would take longer for him to get better. I believed she was coming to the understanding that he might not be able to go back home without twenty-four-hour nursing care, but it was still hard. I tried to encourage her to tell her children that she needed some help, but she wasn't quite ready for that.

I called an old friend on my way home from work to see if she would like to meet for a cold drink. I had been in a non-air-conditioned car in ninety-degree-plus weather, and I knew it was her day off. We caught up with each other's lives as we do, and I asked her how she was getting on, knowing that her ex-husband was on the verge of getting remarried. Our talking turned into some pool time and dinner together at our home.

While she was there my husband visited with her while I took a call from one of my children. My son asked us to pray for a friend's mom who was hospitalized. This friend had practically lived at our house during his junior high years, and I was saddened to learn that his mom was struggling. She had been in a long-term marriage that had ended in divorce and had turned to alcohol for comfort. Her husband, too, was about to be engaged.

My daughter has been grieving the loss to throat cancer of a dear friend and client who had also had her husband leave her. This friend left behind a son who was just finished his first year of college.

Another friend had just been to my house to share that her daughter, who had gotten away from an unhealthy relationship with a man, had just discovered that she was pregnant by him. Another friend had just returned from vacation and told me that she and her husband had gone straight to the hospital, as her dad had suffered a small stroke.

My brother called while my friend was getting ready to leave, and my husband saw her to the car so I could talk to him. He and my sister-in-law were struggling as they were approaching the one-year mark of their son's taking his life. My brother confided that his wife was struggling, and I sensed that he was feeling inadequate in knowing how to help her. I asked him if they were talking to each other, and he said yes and that his wife had agreed that it made her feel better when they did talk about it. He had encouraged her to talk to some parents she'd met who had been through similar circumstances.

I asked my brother how he was doing. He got quiet for a minute and then continued, "I think I'm doing okay, but I had kind of a weird thing happen the other night," he told me. "It was raining really hard, and I had this really sad feeling that Preston was out in the rain, and I should have been able to help him come in and get out of the rain." A lump formed in my throat as I tried to hold back the tears. Why? I guess because I didn't want to add to my brother's pain, but maybe it would have helped him. I don't know. I feel so inadequate in knowing how to help in all these different situations, which is why today I decided the best thing I could do was to just kneel and lay all this pain and hurt at my Savior's feet.

Lord, all of this pain is difficult to know how to deal with. I am clueless, but I know You aren't. You know a lot about pain. You tell us to bring all of our hurt and pain to You and to trust. I may have my whys answered on this earth, or I may not until we are reunited with you, but for now, help us through all the pain.

#ArmorofGod

Now may the Lord of peace himself give you his peace at all times and in every situation. The Lord be with you all.

—2 Thessalonians 3:16 (NLT)

My cousin recently sent me an old photo of me and his sister, my cousin, dressed up when we were small children. She was dressed as Prince Phillip and I was a cowgirl with a cape.

I tried to recall the day the photo was taken. What came to mind was the way she liked to dress up and the feeling that I had been talked into being something so we could enjoy play time together. I would have rather been inside, playing with her Easy-Bake Oven, but that would have bored her to death. We had learned at an early age to compromise a lot, because we enjoyed being together. We were the only two girls out of eight boys who were thrust together on holidays, until years later when two more girl cousins came along.

The picture was even more special and brought tears to my eyes because I had lost this cousin at a very young age. I had just become a mother for the first time and been in my mid-twenties when I learned of her death. I was left with many questions.

When we got together for extended weekends on holidays as teenagers, we really enjoyed getting out from under the thumbs of our parents and riding around together. We would get into some quite serious conversations for such young girls. We had a common Christian legacy in the grandparents that we shared, and while I had gone to church since being in my mother's womb, it wasn't until I attended a teen conference that I came to understand that God was so much more than a distant being who had rules and regulations. So, when I was learning all about this God that cared about me personally, I was sharing with this cousin my new understanding.

I remember her sharing how much she disliked the school that she was going to and how she just didn't feel she fit in. She was more of a tomboy, and I had been a chubby little kid who often felt excluded too, so we had a lot to talk about. I was eager to share with her how God accepted her just as she was.

Because of the great distance between us in later years, me in South Florida and her out East, we didn't stay in touch as much as I would have liked. So when I heard that she was gone, I was quite devastated.

I had always wondered whether she was in heaven, knowing that this isn't based on our goodness. I knew my cousin knew she was sinful. I just didn't have the reassurance that she had trusted in what

Jesus had done for her. The not knowing had always been difficult for me, until that random day that her older brother had decided to forward me that photograph. In it she was wearing a hat with a feather in it. In one hand she held a shield, in the other a sword. I believe without a doubt that God used that photo to assure me that she was with Him. He revealed to me that day what I had been waiting years to know (over fifty years, to be exact). He gave me the peace that she is with Him. In that photo, the armor that she was carrying was what spoke to me. She had in her hand the "shield of faith: to extinguish all the flaming arrows of the evil one" and the "helmet of salvation" and the "sword of the spirit," which is the word of God (Ephesians 6:10–17).

Dear Lord, thank You for giving me reassurance, after all these years, that my dear cousin is in Your presence. Thank You for the years that we did have together, the chatting at all hours of the night, the spiritual conversations we had, and the legacy of the grandparents we shared.

#CalledOut

Those who have been ransomed by the Lord will return. They will enter Jerusalem singing, crowned with everlasting joy. Sorrow and mourning will disappear, and they will be filled with joy and gladness.

—Isaiah 35:10 (NLT)

We've all heard the expression "out of the mouths of babes." When my daughter was a mere thirteen, she taught me a very important life lesson. I was caught by surprise that I hadn't already learned it. I was forty at the time and had lived half of my life. What could this pipsqueak teach me!

I was busy complaining one evening about how difficult life was and how I had "had it"! I was expressing that I couldn't wait until things got simpler, meaning the sale of our home so that we could get our finances in order. We were looking forward to our eldest son moving out of his teen years, and we were anticipating new neighbors whom I thought would be easier to love. She interjected that I would probably never be happy, that it seemed that I had been unhappy most of my life! *Wham!*

Was there any truth to what she was saying? I grew very defensive and tried to justify being unhappy, but her comment haunted me. "Well, life is hard, and I am unhappy about the way a lot of things are going right now, but I don't think I complain that much—or do I? We do have a lot to be thankful for." I guess my actions spoke louder than my words. Ouch.

I woke up the morning after this conversation, and as I read my devotions, it hit me. I was reading in Isaiah about the joy of the redeemed. "Strengthen the feeble hands, steady the knees that give way; say to those with fearful hearts, be strong, do not fear; your God will come, He will come with vengeance; with divine retribution he will come to save you. Then the eyes of the blind will open and the ears of the deaf unstopped. Then will the lame leap like a deer, and the mute tongue shout for joy. Water will gush forth in the wilderness and streams in the desert." (Isaiah 35: 3-6). (NIV) The chapter ended with "They will enter Zion with singing; everlasting Joy will crown their heads." And the best part, "Gladness and Joy will overtake them, and sorrow and sighing will flee away" (Isaiah 35: 10). (NIV)

Life is hard here. I know we are called to "count it all joy." I also know that we can have victory in the midst of sorrow. I have experienced this, but that day I learned that I would have *times of unhappiness.* There will be times of sorrow and sighing. We can have "victory in Jesus" on this earth but not constantly. We will still experience sorrow, and we will feel like sighing because this is not our home.

God wants me to learn to totally "rest" in Him. As a young believer I bought into the misconception that the Christian life would be easier. The older I became, the more I realized that life in general, and the Christian life in particular, becomes more difficult. I thought I had discovered the formula. What I learned was that life is very challenging, and there isn't a formula. I also learned that where I thought I could have victory, I couldn't. Where I never thought I would struggle, I did; where I thought I had solutions, they fell apart.

Where does this leave me? Right in the arms of my loving Heavenly Father, completely at his mercy to show me the way to go home—our real home, that home that will take away all of our sorrow and sighing. My heavenly home.

Thank You, Lord for my daughter and for using her to remind me that this isn't my home. Forgive me for thinking that if everything worked out the way I would like it to that I would be content with this earthly home. Thank You for using my discontentedness to show me that I will always have struggles here. Help me not to be surprised when they come. I pray that You will use my complaining to reveal to our daughter that this isn't her home either!

#CantStopCrying

You turned my wailing into dancing; you removed my sackcloth and clothed me with joy, that my heart may sing to you and not be silent. O Lord my God, I will give you thanks forever.

—Psalm 30:11 (NIV)

Wailing is defined as a long, loud, high-pitched cry, as of grief or pain.

Maybe you have grieved over the loss of an immediate family

member or, as a mom, grieved the loss of hope for children, the disappointment being so great that the wailing came.

I was reminded of my own experiences of grief when a friend called in tears recently to ask me to pray for her. I remembered asking friends to pray for me when I was too distraught and weary to pray. I had been in her place, and because I was reminded of the gut-wrenching pain, I stopped and prayed she would find relief from her sorrow and peace in the middle of it. I prayed for her child, that God would work in their life, and that she would find the wisdom a parent needs in order to know when and when not to help.

The Psalmist's words that encouraged me will encourage her as well, and her wailing will turn into dancing. But for now, just let the tears flow!

Lord, I can't take away the heartache of my shopping buddy and friend at this moment, but I know that You can and will, and I know that at that moment she will experience a wardrobe makeover unlike any treasure we could find in a department store. She will be clothed with joy indescribable, and it will be in Your perfect timing!

#DestinationSet

Do not let your hearts be troubled. Trust in God, trust also in me. In my Father's house are many rooms; if it were not so I would have told you. I am going there to prepare a place for you. And if I go and prepare a place for you, I will come back and take you to be with me that you also may be where I am. You know the way to the place where I am going." Jesus comforts His disciples.

—John 14: 1–4 (NIV)

I had a problem with a toe after I had been convinced by a

professional to undergo a routine procedure that would rule out ever having to worry about an ingrown nail again. Nine months later (the length of a pregnancy!) and two nail removals behind me, along with talk of surgery, I decided to get a second opinion.

It is amazing how painful a toe can be and how the discomfort can become such a focus that it is hard to think of anything else but that throbbing toe. It reminds me of the old cartoons where you see the toe get hit by an object, and the pain starts radiating. Knowing that I was not going to be able to solve this problem alone or with the help of my husband, I contacted a doctor who had come highly recommended by several people and asked if his staff could somehow fit me into their schedule. Because the toe had been on my mind all night, I called within minutes of climbing out of bed. I expected to hear an answering machine that would tell me their office hours so I could promptly call at that time. Much to my surprise, they answered at 7:30 and said that if I could get there by 8:15 they could fit me in! The receptionist was very kind and started giving me directions to the office by naming landmarks, etc. I knew in my mind exactly where their building was located.

I threw on my clothes, brushed my teeth, ran a brush through my hair, and was out that door by 8 a.m. My husband offered to drive me, as the toe had become such a problem that he had been my advocate on the last couple of appointments. I was explaining to him how to get there, naming one landmark after another as we got closer. Remembering how I had found the town confusing when we'd moved here just ten years ago, I was saying how really nice it was when you were familiar with an area and when listening to directions could follow them quite easily, as you knew all the places they were talking about. I ended what my husband probably found to be mindless conversation (especially this early in the morning) with, "It is really nice to know where you're going!"

My husband looked at me and then repeated what I'd said: "Yes, it really is nice to know where you're going!"

I didn't have to say anything and neither did he, a case for the beauty of being married for thirty-seven years. We instantly smiled at each other and rested in the moment of being reminded that sore toes and aches and pains would all come to a screeching halt the minute we took our last breaths on this earth. Yes, this sore toe was a huge inconvenience, but instantly things had been put into perspective for us, in the larger picture of our future home. I don't exactly know how I'll get there, but it is clear that once this life is over my new life in Christ will begin. I won't even need to use my GPS, because He will be the travel agent of all travel agents. Thanks for the reminder!

Lord, I thank You that we can live this life with the assurance of spending our eternity with You. Thank You for the people that You put in my life to share Your words with me so I could come to that point in my life. Help us to endure all that You have for us throughout the years, and use us now, when our bodies still have some miles on them, and also when they are worn out. I've been the recipient of much encouragement from many of Your people in their later years. Their bodies are worn but their spirits are alive!

#FutureCertain

> No eye has seen, no ear has heard, no mind has conceived what God has prepared for those who love him — but God has revealed it to us by his Spirit.
>
> —1 Corinthians 2:9–10 (NLT)

There is a house I pass on my routine walks and bicycle rides, a rustic little house on a little canal. It looks very homey, and there is a little sign that hangs from their eave that reads Almost Heaven.

Because my husband loves to fish, we bought a home on a canal. That way he can step into his boat and be out on the water in just a few moments. When we moved into this house many years ago, a dear friend gave me a pillow that reads, "Heaven seems a little closer in a house beside the water." Though it is worn and has lost its color, I keep it, because it is a reminder of the friend who gave it to me but also a reminder that after I take my last breath on this earth my life will go on, albeit it in a much different form. I will live for an eternity with my Creator and Savior.

It is good to know that you know that you know your destiny after this life ends, and it is especially comforting, when you have had family or friends leave this earth, to know that they live on as believers, trusting in Jesus Christ.

What would heaven look like to you? Maybe it would have lots of water so that you could fish in solitude all day. Maybe it would be a place with friends and family visiting all day; maybe it would be one continuous tennis match, without growing weary; or maybe it would be a sightseeing vacation, looking at the marvels of Creation. Whatever your idea is, you will not be disappointed. Our ideas of heaven are pretty limited and a poor imitation of what it will really be like. Our experiences, however much we have been able to travel this world, only give us a glimpse as to what it will be like.

My muddy little canal, while pleasant to sit by with my husband as we rest and reflect about our, lives, isn't even close to meeting the "living water" face to face. Although I can put our boat into the water, I cannot swim in it. But the water available to us is described by Jesus to the Samaritan women at the well: "Everyone who drinks this water will be thirsty again, but whoever drinks the water I give him will never thirst. Indeed, the water I give him will become in him a spring of water welling up to eternal life." John 4: 13,14 (NIV)

Based on God's word, artists have tried to capture what it will look like, and authors have tried to put it into words, but it can't be done.

Are you confident that when you leave this earth you will spend Eternity with your Creator? I was asked that question one time and I did not have that assurance. In fact, I believed the people asking me were arrogant to think that they could know. But the difference was that they knew the scripture that made it clear that you *can* know. I did not know it until they shared it with me. I'd like to share it with you; it's John 5:13. "I write these things to you who believe in the name of the Son of God so that you may *know* that you have eternal life."

John 3:16 says it all: "For God so loved the world that he gave his one and only Son, that whoever believes in him shall not perish but have eternal life." (NIV) and Ephesians 2:8, 9 says "For it is by grace that you have been saved, through faith---and this is not from yourselves, it is the gift of God....not by works, so that no one can boast." (NIV)

Lord, I thank you that we don't have to just hope but can know for sure that we will spend eternity with you after our job is done on this earth—not because of what we have done or not done but because of you taking on our sin for us so that we can be reconciled to you. When we walk and talk with you, the living water, we can indeed get a glimpse of heaven!

#ItisWhatitis

God replied to Moses, "I AM WHO I AM. Say this to the people of Israel: I AM has sent me to you." God also said to Moses, "Say this to the people of Israel: Yahweh, the God of your ancestors—the God of Abraham, the God of Isaac, and the God of Jacob—has sent me to you. This is my eternal name, my name to remember for all generations."

—Exodus 3:14–15 (NLT)

I was planning a trip to Arizona to take my eighty-eight-year-old mother and fourteen-year-old granddaughter to visit my brother and sister-in-law and nephews and to take a girls' trip to see the Grand Canyon.

Before we left I went to an urologist, as I'd had a UTI that was a little different than most I had experienced. One test showed nothing, and my doctor wanted to schedule an ultrasound of my kidneys to check for stones when I got home.

When I returned home, I almost canceled it, as I wasn't having any symptoms of kidney stones. My husband encouraged me to just go ahead and have it checked.

When the doctor came into the room and looked at the images, I could tell that there was something significant in what he was looking at. Sure enough, he informed us there was a shadow that was of concern, and he scheduled a CT scan.

My husband went with me to learn the results of the scan, and we were told there was a tumor on my right kidney, which the doctor said was most likely renal cell cancer. This doctor had the best bedside manner and could even say the dreaded word *cancer* without causing alarm. He and my husband looked together at the images as he explained his plan to remove the kidney.

That night my husband and I decided to go out to eat, to relax while we digested the news.

There was a small arts and craft show in our downtown area, so after dinner we decided to take a stroll and look.

One vendor was selling coastal-looking signs with different sayings on them in fun tropical colors. They caught my eye, so we approached his booth. As we walked up to the booth, the man asked me, "Are you feeling lucky today?"

I chuckled to myself as I looked at my husband's reaction, in light of the news we had just received. I said, "Sure I'm feeling lucky!" He then explained that there was a sign with the word *Free* written on the back. If I was lucky enough to pick that particular sign, it was mine!

So my husband and I started looking around, reading the different signs, and there was one that caught our attention. It said,

"It Is What It Is." It came in different colors, and I chose my favorite color, green. The man looked a bit amazed. He picked it up, turned it around, and showed me the word *Free!* When he asked why I'd picked that one, I told him that I had received some not very good news that day and that it had seemed appropriate. One woman standing there overheard my story, and she came up and gave me a great big hug! I just know that God sets up these situations to assure us that He is walking through everything with us.

So we went home and hung our sign as a reminder that we have no control over the situation and to remind us that God is most assuredly walking with us.

I since have had my kidney removed, and another CT scan has shown that the cancer isn't in any of my other organs. So for now things are good. My doctor said there isn't anything I can't do. I should just live my life, which I plan on doing. I do have to follow up with an oncologist every six months to be monitored. It's just another reminder that only He knows our days on this earth. None of us know how long we have, and we just have to live one day at a time.

It's funny how often I hear that expression since I got that sign. I was talking with a friend who is going through a difficult time during which she has no control over the outcome. She sighed and said, "It is what it is." The same day a neighbor who was in the process of remodeling his kitchen was frustrated, as their island had not been placed exactly where it was supposed to be, which was making the space between the island and the refrigerator tighter. When I asked him if he could have it moved, he explained that it had been screwed into their new wood floor and that "it is what it is"! We, having just remodeled our kitchen, had a similar experience. The wrong cabinet style was ordered, and the color of the island was quite a bit different than the sample we'd looked at. At first I was really frustrated, but once things were in place, it looked fine. The man who'd ordered it would have had to take it out of his own pocket to fix the mistake, and my husband wasn't going to do that. I, on the other hand, thought we should have gotten what we ordered and was ready to insist it be changed, but my logical husband convinced me that it wasn't that big of a deal, that the relationship with the man was more important. He was right, and so, "it is what it is."

We seem to use the saying when we don't like what is happening and it is clear that we have absolutely no control over the situation or there is really no solution to change the outcome.

We have no control over many things in our lives, but Jesus, who made it clear that he is equal to God the Father, is a Sovereign God who is in complete control over everything that happens. So when you get discouraged or don't like the outcome of something in your life, remember and be encouraged that "it is what it is." But more importantly, remember what Jesus says: "I Am Who I Am"

Jesus, I thank You that, while many things don't turn out as we would choose, You do tell us that You work all things together for our good. Yes, even the timing of our deaths. You are the great I AM and You can heal, but I realize that in Your sovereignty, You can choose not to heal me here but in my eternal home. If that is the case, it will "be what it will be," but I will be with You, the great I AM!

#NewLife

The man from whom the demons had gone out begged to go with him, but Jesus sent him away, saying, "Return home and tell how much God has done for you." So the man went away and told all over town how much Jesus had done for him.

—Luke: 8:37 (MSG)

I had been working a lot and decided to take a day to have a bit of my kind of fun, which included heading to one of my favorite discount clothing stores to browse all by myself.

I love to look at notepaper, etc., and as I was turning down this particular aisle, I saw a woman who was lingering in the aisle that I wanted to look in. I waited, thinking she would move on, but when she didn't, I decided to just look alongside her. She was obviously struggling with making a decision. When she noticed me there, she asked, "Which one do you think my husband would like?" She had picked up some leather covers for Bibles and was trying to decide which one her husband would like better.

I gave her my opinion and then asked, "Are those Bible covers?" She affirmed, and I asked her whether she was a believer.

This one question and her answer led to a mutual understanding, and she opened up to me about her life. She started to share in her Haitian dialect, "I was in a really bad place, and I was really messed up. I had some really bad things happen to me. I did some really bad things." She continued. "I was into voodoo, but Jesus changed me; He turned my life around!"

Sensing that she was dwelling a lot on her past, I said, "Yes, but remember, Jesus remembers your sin no more. It is separated as far as the east from the west.

She smiled and said, "I know." We moved on to all that God was doing in her life now—the believer husband who had been brought into her life and how he had walked with her and encouraged her, her two precious children, and her prayers for them. We ended our conversation and agreed that if we never saw each other again in this life we would for certain somehow recognize each other in heaven.

Thank You, Lord for putting this dear woman, literally, in my path today. Thanks for this woman's willingness to share what You have done in her life. Continue to use her in this way. Thanks for using her to encourage me and reminding me today that there is never anyone too far gone or too involved in destructive or even satanic behavior for You to reach and change their lives forever!

#PrepareHimRoom

For a child is born to us, a son is given to us.
The government will rest on his shoulders. And
he will be called: Wonderful Counselor, Mighty
God, Everlasting Father, Prince of Peace. His
government and its peace will never end. He will
rule with fairness and justice from the throne of
his ancestor David for all eternity. The passionate
commitment of the Lord of Heaven's Armies will
make this happen!

—Isaiah 9:6–7 (NLT)

It was eleven days before Christmas, and while I was almost
finished with what I could do ahead of time, I had that little nagging
feeling that I was forgetting something or someone who I really
wanted to remember this season.

Three of our grandchildren were coming tonight! We planned
to celebrate an early Christmas with them. The gifts were wrapped,
the cookie dough was mixed, ready to do cutouts, and my husband
had figured out dinner. Normally I would make something, but
with this time of year comes winter colds, and I had just gotten on
an antibiotic and was feeling a bit under the weather.

A friend, who is a grandma too, was bringing her grandson
over to fish off our dock and to possibly participate in the cookie
decorating. When I thought about them coming over, I remembered
how dirty the gazebo was where we hang out while the fishing is
going on. So I got out my bleach and rags and spruced it up, put
a holly tablecloth on, and substituted the blue candle with a red
candle. Voila—I was ready for the celebrations to begin!

As I was scrubbing away, I was thinking of the reason we all go
to such lengths to prepare for the arrival of Christmas day. I stopped
to get out my piano music and sing and play "Joy to the World"!

Joy to the world;
The Lord is come!
Let earth receive her King.
Let every heart prepare Him room;
And heaven and nature sing,
and heaven and nature sing,
and heaven, and heaven, and nature sing.

"Prepare Him room." Among my preparations for Christmas is the nativity scene that my grandfather built over fifty years ago. When my grandparents were in their later years that is the only decoration they would put out. I am older now and have been simplifying; I, also, have found that it is my most precious decoration. My grandfather put a Christmas light in the back of the stable so the light shines right on our Savior. When I am going about my preparations, I turn that light on to focus on what the season is really about. I was reminded of how messy that stable had been, how nothing had gone according to plan. There hadn't been any room for the Savior, and yet out of the dirt and filth and mess had come the greatest hope the world has ever known!

I decided to take a break to grab a bite to eat. I turned on the TV and saw a special news report that there had just been a shooting at an elementary school in Connecticut. It was 12-14-12. There weren't any details yet, but I was reminded again in a tragic way how the sting of our sinful hearts messes up our lives and the lives of others. In that same announcement came a news story about a woman being set on fire. Oh Lord, we need you—every hour, every minute we need you!

No amount of precaution or preparation can stop the darkness that happens in this broken world. I'm guessing that nagging feeling was the call to lift up those families that had just found out they had lost a loved one, as well as the families of the shooter, who didn't see this tragedy coming either. I now know who I want to remember this season. They don't know me, and I don't know them, but I do know that we have the same Savior. My gift to them will be to cry out on their behalf for the Great Comforter to touch them and heal them.

Lord, forgive me for being whiney about how this Christmas will be different than all the other Christmases that I remember, when our entire family was together. We may never experience Christmases like those we recall while we were raising our children, with all of us together. But there are people who are really hurting this year. My brother and sister-in-law are struggling with their son's absence from their family's festivities and are having a difficult time with wanting to make any preparations. Lord, please reveal Yourself and bring comfort to my immediate family and the families going through the tragedy that is unfolding right now. Be with the lonely, and the grieving, and the brokenhearted. Help us to focus on You and the joy You brought the night You came to save us from our sin-torn world and sin-filled selves. Life is messy, but Lord, prepare our hearts for You, fill the hurts and voids, and help us to praise you in spite of our circumstances. We are reminded that this is really not our home. Without You, we, and the whole world, are hopeless. But in You we have everything we need, including the promise of eternal life when we leave this broken world that You came to heal. We can't prepare for everything, but we can prepare our hearts for You. You will take us, in your timing, to the room You have prepared for us!

#Purple

They put a purple robe on him then twisted together
a crown of thorns and set it on him.

—Mark 15:17 (NIV)

My father-in-law had passed away, so it had been a busy couple of weeks. When a friend called to see whether I wanted to get out, I jumped at the opportunity.

I showered and dressed and threw on some clothes. I'm typically not drawn to purple for clothing, but I happened to put on a purple top that day. Soon my friend arrived at the door, and we were ready to go. We both noticed that, coincidentally, she had happened to wear purple as well. We agreed it must be a purple kind of day.

Just as we were heading out, my husband received a phone call from the funeral home where they had taken care of his father's arrangements. They were letting him know that his dad's cremains were ready and could be picked up. I could tell that he was dreading the task. My friend piped up and asked him if he would like us to stop by and get them. He was relieved, and so we made the funeral home our first stop.

After giving them my father-in-law's name, we waited, not knowing quite what to expect. In a few minutes they came out carrying a box with his remains—wrapped in a purple velvet bag! Today was indeed turning into a purple day.

I just knew that this was one of those moments when God was making it beyond clear that He was walking with us. He was assuring us that my husband's dad, who had come to a relationship with Christ in his late eighties, was now with the King of Kings! Purple, the color of royalty!

I was recently reminded of this story when one of our sons, who had just purchased his first home, started speaking of a purple mattress that he had ordered online. Being in a career that kept him on the water for months at a time, he hadn't had his own bed for almost ten years! He was sharing with us his excitement about this new *purple* mattress that he had ordered. He couldn't wait for it to arrive so he could get his first good night's rest on it. It was advertised as the world's first no-pressure mattress. There is a Youtube video about the mattress, which shows their raw-egg test. His brother thinks that the Goldilocks in the video is what sold him. I must admit the advertising was great, and she was pretty cute! They ship the mattresses free of charge to your front door, and yes, it arrives in none other than a purple container!

He was so concerned that it might arrive before he had to go back on the tug, but one day when we got home, what did we see on the front porch by his front door but his "purple"! It was pretty exciting to unwrap it and watch it unroll and expand into its sleepy shape! We all climbed onto the "purple" and just lay there and rested in the comfort of it for a moment. As the day went on and we were busy with tasks around his house, we were all getting sleepy, and our son started saying "pu-u-u-u-r-r-r-rple." It has become a catchphrase now with my husband and me when it is time for bed: pu-u-u-u-r-r-r-r-rple. There is nothing like your own bed, but the purple takes a comfortable bed to the next level!

I think the company picked the right color for their product. The color denotes wealth and royalty, a mattress fit for a king. I have always marveled that in God's great design we lie down and are essentially motionless for some eight hours.

During our waking hours we can come to Him to find rest. "Come to me, all you who are weary and burdened, and I will give you rest" (Matthew 11:28 NIV). During our nightly rest we can sleep on our "purple," which may be the ultimate in rest here on this earth. When our lives here are over, we can't take our "purple" with us, but if we are resting in the work of Christ, the rest in the life to follow will be a rest that is beyond our human comprehension. "What no eye has seen, what no ear has heard, and what no human mind has conceived"—the things God has prepared for those who love him (1 Corinthians 2:9 NIV).

It will be an unparalleled rest with the King of King and Lord of Lords, where there will be rest from our labors (Revelation 14:13) and, I have a feeling, a lot of purple!

Dear Lord, Some days can be so long. I thank You that in Your wisdom You knew that these fragile bodies would need rest and designed our bodies to require it. Thank You for making it clear that we cannot just hope but know for certain that we can count on resting with You for an eternity, based on our faith and trust in Your paying the price so that we could be reconciled with God.

#SourceofPeace

> We're all sin-infected, sin-contaminated. Our best efforts are grease-stained rags.
>
> —Isaiah 64:6 (MSG)

After a busy week of activities, which included being around and interacting with a lot of different people, I intentionally kept Friday open so that I could be at home by myself to do some spring cleaning.

I started outside with my bleach and sponges and rags and bucket to spruce up our outside gazebo, one of my favorite places to be "still" and rest. I certainly wasn't doing any resting; I was busy removing mold and mildew and scrubbing every square inch so it would be restored to its shiny white surface. I continued, filling a spray bottle with "outside" bleach and spraying the mold that was on the patio area before I moved on to a set of Adirondack chairs.

I thought about calling a detailer to do my husband's boat, to surprise him, but I decided not to spend the money right then. I wasn't ready to take on that big a project myself.

I moved inside and decided to tackle my notepaper, stationary, and card drawer. I am a member of a card club of sorts. As the cards come in monthly, they pile up quickly if I am not diligent to file them. I was also going through the ones that were without envelopes, matching them to envelopes that would fit, and sorting through some cards that I had held onto for some time and for some reason hadn't sent.

In my mess of cards, I ran across several cards that I recognized. One was the program from my dad's memorial service two and a half years ago. The picture that was on the program was of him in his later years. I found myself fighting back tears as I looked at his picture and realized how much I missed him. I read the scripture that was underneath his picture; it was from Romans 8:38–39. "For I am convinced that neither death nor life, neither angels nor demons, neither the present nor the future, not any powers, neither height nor depth, nor anything else in all creation, will be able to separate us from the love of God that is in Christ Jesus our Lord." I needed to be reminded of this, not only for my dad but for myself, as I had been through quite a discouraging week. That week I would have loved to run some things past my dad, but of course I couldn't. So I took the words beneath his name as his wisdom for me this day.

One card in particular stood out to me. I remembered the day I'd purchased it. On the front was a picture of an Adirondack chair with a few shells on the armrest. It was sitting beside a shoreline, with the waves lapping up against the legs of the chair. I think Adirondack chairs are synonymous with resting, and I remembered why the picture had drawn me to this card. But for some reason, as much as I like to send cards, I'd never sent this one. It was bent on the edges and slightly discolored from age, but still I hadn't been able to toss it in the wastebasket where I had been throwing other cards that I knew I wouldn't use. I remembered that when I'd bought it I'd been thinking what a beautiful card it was and how it would be such an encouragement to some special friend. Little did I know that, although it was too damaged to send, my Savior knew I would need to be reminded this very day of His words. So it was as if He were sending this card to me personally. I stopped, and I read. The words, PEACE, WORLD, and HEART were in bold and in larger print.

PEACE I leave with you, my peace I give unto you: not as the WORLD giveth, give me unto you. Let not your HEART be troubled, neither let it be afraid" (John 14:27). May the Lord keep you today in perfect peace. I stopped and looked at the card again. I reread the words, words so familiar but ones that I needed so desperately to hear that day. I felt as if my earthly father and my Heavenly Father had both spoken to me.

Damaged is what we are, having no value apart from Christ. We are dirty and moldy, like my gazebo, until we are "scrubbed up" by the master "detailer."

Lord, thank You for being a God of details, a God who loves me so much that You saw to it today that I had word not only from my earthly father but from you, my Heavenly Father, as well. You both pointed me to Yourself, the only place to find peace. Not only are my gazebo and patio all spruced up for the spring, I am reminded that your righteousness has made me as white as snow and that when you look at me, a daughter of the most High King, you see me completely righteous, because of what you did.

DEDICATION AND SPECIAL THANKS

To my niece, Shelby, for her encouragement to complete this book and her help in organizing the content.

To my eldest son for the cover design, for sharing his creative marketing skill set and insight, which is within his giftedness.

When I think back over my life, I know I was greatly influenced by men who shared the word of God from the pulpit, or over radio waves, or in book form. Robert S. McGee, author of *The Search for Significance*, was a huge influence in pointing me toward using God's word rather than my feelings to navigate life. I have shared his teaching material, to encourage other young mommas to listen to God's word more and more and to their feelings less and less.

When I think of pastors who truly were personal pastors in my life, I think of Bill and Mary Katherine Colclasure, of Pine Ridge Church (PCA) in Orlando and David and Susan Lane, Edgewater Alliance Church in Edgewater, Florida. I share their wives' names as well, because my husband and I received great encouragement and wisdom, shared from God's word, from both these men and their wives, who were a big part of their ministries.

Another pastor who had great influence in my life was Steve Brown, author, teacher at Key Life Network and a seminary professor. His honest discussions of the depth of our sinfulness helped me come to a more realistic view of myself and thus a greater understanding of the truly amazing grace that I received from God through the sacrifice of his son, Jesus Christ.

Dr. James Dobson, psychologist, author, radio broadcaster, and founder of *Focus on the Family*, was my lifeline when I was a mom of infants and toddlers. Luckily, his broadcast would come on when I was in the waiting line to pick up my two oldest children from preschool and elementary school. As a mom of four, I really don't know whether I would have survived without his encouragement. His broadcasts were like fuel to help me get through many of my tough parenting days.

Dr. D. James Kennedy, founder of Coral Ridge Presbyterian Church in Fort Lauderdale, Florida, presented messages from the word of God in such a way that God was elevated to where He deserves to be. His messages from the word of God were challenging and convincing.

Charles "Chuck" Swindoll, whom I often listened to on his Bible-teaching radio ministry, *Insight for Living*, has the ability to take God's word and teach me how to apply it. He has shared his heart and life with thousands on the radio. Though I have never personally met Chuck, I feel as though I know him because he has walked me through some tough situations through teaching me the application of God's word.

I'd like to thank my parents, Robert and Jacqueline Kinney, for taking me to church so that I could hear the word of God over and over again. Also my maternal grandparents, Roscoe and Lura Dunnuck, for tangibly showing me their commitment to their Savior by reading devotionals with me, writing scripture on their kitchen blackboard, and dropping everything to visit with me when I'd pop in with my friends. I'm also grateful for the gift they gave me—my first modern-language Bible—as a high school graduation gift. They made me feel like the most special granddaughter they had; I know they had three others!

Special thanks to the many girlfriends who God brought into my life throughout all my different stages of parenting. They were like the sisters I never had. Their willingness to patiently and tirelessly listen as I worked through tough parenting issues contributed to my survival and sanity. Barbara, Bobra, Dale, Diane, Francesca, Jeanette, Joy, Joyce, Kathy, Linda, Nona, Tammy, and Vicki, I couldn't have survived without your listening ears and compassion. I like to call you my "baker's dozen" of girlfriends—you listened, sympathized, counseled, and gave me real help as well throughout all the stages of parenting and life in general.

I want to give special thanks to each of our four children, who were temporarily loaned to my husband and me. Without you, this book would never have been written. The lessons I have learned from each of you have been numerous and are ongoing. I have loved being together as a family doing this life together. I have treasured in my heart all the stories of your lives as we've sat around the dinner table, sharing the best and the worst parts of our days. I have loved celebrating all of your individual accomplishments and the infectious laughter that came with much of the storytelling. Thank you for putting up with an imperfect mom and loving me in spite of myself. I'm even thankful for the heartache and tears that have brought me prostrate before my God. It was during those times that my Savior showed up through scripture, to comfort me in the way that only He can, assuring me that He is walking with me until He calls me home.

Last, but not least, I'd like to recognize my brother and sister-in-love for their unwavering faith in the midst of an unthinkable trial (the loss of their son, Preston). They wake each day continuing to trust in the goodness of their Savior. Your lives and resilience give me and others hope that no matter how dark our journeys, God is faithful to his children. Your joy in the midst of horrific circumstances affirms the truth in Philippians 4:7 (NLT): "Then you will experience God's peace, which exceeds anything we can understand. His peace will guard your hearts and minds as you live in Christ Jesus."

Printed in the United States
By Bookmasters